How to Be Happier in the Job You Sometimes Can't Stand

HOW TO BE HAPPIER IN THE JOB YOU SOMETIMES CAN'T STAND

ROSS WEST

BROADMAN PRESS
NASHVILLE, TENNESSEE

ISBN: 0-8054-6018-7
Dewey Decimal Classification: 650.1
Subject heading: JOB SATISFACTION
Library of Congress Catalog Card Number: 90-38838
Printed in the United States of America

Library of Congress Cataloging-in-Publication Data
West, Ross, 1943-
    How to be happier in the job you sometimes can't stand / Ross West.
      p.   cm.
    Includes bibliographical references.
    ISBN 0-8054-6018-7
    1. Job satisfaction.   I. Title.
HF5549.5 J63W45   1991
650.1—dc20   90-38838
                                                                   CIP

CONTENTS

Preface 7
1. Give Your Job the Place It Deserves. 11
2. Focus On Reality 22
3. Think Creatively About Your Job 36
4. Build Positive Relationships 47
5. Handle Criticism Carefully 62
6. Master the Tension of Stress. 75
7. Get Organized. 98
8. Decide to Grow 112
9. Live with Balance 126
10. Let Happiness Catch You 138
Postscript: What If None of These Ideas
Make Enough Difference. 148
Bibliography 155

Preface

Do you need some help being happier in your work? You're not alone. Almost every time I get into a conversation that heads down a halfway-serious track, unhappiness at work turns out to be a major theme.

I hear this unhappiness in the voices of people who do all sorts of work and whose ages are varied. These people may be married or single, childless or with children. Some of these people are male, and some are female. Some are in management, and some are not. The particular status in life doesn't seem to matter.

A measure of unhappiness at work characterizes these folks, however else they may be different. Sometimes that measure of unhappiness is full and overflowing.

Maybe it's because my antennae are out, listening especially for conversations that reveal difficulties at work. Maybe it's just that I'm drawn to folks who are experiencing unhappiness at work. But I think there's more to it than that.

Beyond casual conversations, I've done some research in the area of job satisfaction. I've begun to feel that lots of folks could use help in being happier in their jobs, jobs they sometimes just can't stand. Some of these folks have the kinds of jobs of which dreams are made, or at least they appear to be from the outside looking in. But these dream jobs have started looking like nightmares to them.

So, I wrote this book out of my personal observation of and concern for people who seemed to lack sufficient happiness in their work. These people are good people—many of them bright and talented, with much to offer. You'd think they wouldn't need much help in finding more happiness in their work. But they do. You'd think they have it made. But they don't. At least *they* don't think so.

Another reason I wrote this book is that I am on a personal quest to find more happiness in my own work. (There. The news is out.) Maybe you won't think me too brash or boastful if I suggest that I identify with my description of the people I have given in the preceding paragraph. I'm fairly bright, I do have some talents, and I'm oriented toward achievement. At least some folks would think I have a pretty good position, if not the stuff of which dreams are made. Then why don't I have more joy in my work? I needed the answers myself, and so I started looking. This book compiles some of the answers I've discovered and am trying to put into practice. Note that the title of this book is *not* "How to Be *Happy* in the Job You Sometimes Can't Stand." Being perfectly happy all the time in that sort of job is a contradiction. It won't happen, no matter what you do, even if you read this book and do perfectly, day in and day out, everything it advises.

Furthermore, you're unlikely to find a job in which everything—*everything*—is perfect *all* the time, unless you own the company. In fact, I have friends who *do* own their own company, and they're not happy all the time either, in spite of what you read of the attraction of being in business for yourself. The chances are close to 100 percent that you won't find a job of any sort that doesn't have something in it that you just can't stand.

I want to assure you, though, that the ten big ideas in this book *will* help you be *happier* in your job. These ten ideas *will* help you improve your life at work. If you give attention to these ideas, you may not be able to be deliriously happy in your present work. That may be asking too much of any job or any book, and I'm not promising delirious happiness. OK?

You may well be able to be a whole lot happier in your job than you are right now, though. These ten ideas are practical, sound, and helpful. They're not quick fixes, but they will work from the very first day you decide to put them into practice. They have helped me, and I think they will help you.

They will help you *IF*—and that's a bigger-than-usual "if," purposely—you remember that the only sure-fire formula to success is expressed in these two words: "Nothing works." Plans don't work, advice doesn't work, ideas don't work, books don't work. *You* will have to do the work. Just reading this book won't do the job of helping you be happier in your work. Actions are called for. So, in addition to your reading the book, I hope you'll put into practice the guidance and encouragement in the ten helpful ideas in this book.

A major theme of this book, in fact, is that to be happier in our jobs we need to focus on, act on, and make the best of whatever part of our jobs is open to us to control or at least influence. Don't worry so much about what you can't control. Focus on what you *can* control. That may seem to be precious little, I admit. I suspect you will discover you can influence more of your job than you think you can right now, though. If nothing else, you can control how you react to what seems to control you. You may not be able to control many, many aspects of your work that keep you from being happier, but you *can* control how you feel about and react to such things.

One more word—I'm pulling for you. Life is too short—and the time you spend at your job is too long—for you not to take steps to be happier in your job, even if you sometimes can't stand it. You're right. There's *got* to be something better than what you're feeling in your present job. These ten ideas for being happier in your work can help you find it. Applying these ideas may well help you be happier in the job you sometimes can't stand.

1

Give Your Job the Place It Deserves

I just love to see the lights come on." That's what Ed said about his job with the city electric company. One of Ed's duties was to repair the electric lines on stormy nights. Ed and his fellow workers often spent all night repairing the lines during and after a raging storm.

Lights would be off all over the city. Ed went out and worked, though, in spite of cold weather, rainy weather, snowy weather. The job was sometimes dangerous in addition to being downright inconvenient. It had to be done, though.

When Ed came home, he would be soaking wet, chilled, and bone-tired. Ed's wife would tell him how worried about him she had been. Ed would say, "Don't worry about me. I'm okay. And besides, I just love to see the lights come on."

When I heard that true story, a light went on in my head. "I just love to see the lights come on," Ed had said. What a wonderful way to view one's work! Here was a person who found joy in his work, even though perhaps he—like you, like me—could hardly stand it sometimes.

"I just love to see the lights come on." Wouldn't having such a feeling about your own work be great? The first action I'd like to encourage you to take to enable you to find more joy in your job is this: *Give your job the place it deserves.* Here are some ways to do that.

Be Thankful: Your Job Helps You

For a time in my adult life, I was out of a job. I had a wife and a child beginning first grade. I enjoyed good health —physically, mentally, emotionally, and spiritually. I had seven years education beyond high school. I had a college degree and a professional degree, with excellent grades on both transcripts. I had a good work history, having done a creditable job in two positions. I had a problem, however. I had no job.

With all the pluses in my life, that one minus—no job— was the reality that dominated my days. My wife was doing substitute teaching in various schools in the city, and so the family had some income. *I* had no job, though, and that frustration gnawed at me considerably. Although I had a measure of assurance that things eventually would work out, that feeling could not lessen my problem—I had no job. My self-respect slipped a little farther down every day. My sense of identity—and with it my sense of self-worth—was closely intertwined with my work.

I have had many days when I was very unhappy with my work, for various reasons. Perhaps I thought I had too much work to do. Perhaps upline management made demands I felt were unfair or out of harmony with my values. Perhaps I saw little opportunity for creativity, little value in what I was doing, and little prospect for remedying the situation.

On such days, when I have been at my best, I sometimes have been able to force myself to recall those months when I had *no* work, *no* upline management, *no* unfair (or fair) demands, *no* opportunity for creativity, because I had *no* job, period. When I have recalled that dismal time, I have been able to see again the value of having a job. The job may not be all a person wishes it to be, but at least it's a job. When a person is out of work, he or she is more grateful for whatever work can be found. My personal experience and my knowledge of more than one person in this situation verifies that truth.

Being thankful for a job that is not all you thought it would be—or think it ought to be—is not easy. But being thankful for a job encourages the enjoyment of it. A person may not be able to enjoy a job even when he or she *is* thankful for it, but that person probably won't be able to enjoy the job if he or she is *not* thankful for it.

A job is valuable from the standpoint of maintaining self-respect. A job is valuable, too, for providing financial resources. My experience of being out of work stamped that realization indelibly on my mind. When I was out of work, I, a young husband and father, had a clear-eyed vision of one important fact. *A job provides the financial resources needed for living.* We were spending at a surprisingly fast pace the meager savings we had, and little was coming in to replace the money going out.

Most people depend on their jobs to provide the financial where-with-all for living. They may hope their ship will come in. They may dream it will arrive in the form of a multimillion-dollar check through no effort of their own —from a magazine sweepstakes perhaps. They may fantasize that some rich relative they never heard of will show up and endow them for life. They may think it would be nice not to have to work for a living. Almost everybody dreams of cashing in on some get-rich-quick scheme or other and "having it made."

Reality sets in for most of us, however. The clock goes off, awaking us from a too-brief sleep. We get up, and we head to work. As the bumper sticker message goes, "I-O, I-O, So Off to Work I Go." And, when the paychecks are handed out, the bills come due, and we have almost enough money to pay the bills, we are glad to have a job. When we are thinking clearly, we understand that adults support themselves and their families by working, like it or not.

Be Thankful: Your Job Helps Others

You may not think going out in the middle of the night, in stormy weather, to fix lights, is that big a deal. You probably don't put the work Ed did for the electric company— even on stormy nights—in the same class as brain surgery, say, or discovering a cure for cancer. People who repair electric lines don't get the "Nobel Prize for Benefit to Humanity." Maybe they should be in the running, however. When's the last time your home had no electricity? If it's been recently, you can well appreciate the work of folks like Ed.

I'd like to encourage you to think of how your job helps others—immediately or eventually. Admittedly, getting this perspective on our work is a little hard for many of us. All too few people today are able to see the result of the work they do. They sometimes are not able to see how their job directly benefits anybody living or dead. Workers on the assembly line or in the office often do not see the finished product of the work they do. They certainly don't see the person actually getting the benefit of the part of the product she has assembled or completed the paperwork on.

That's unfortunate. We will get more joy out of our jobs, even the jobs we can't stand, if we will focus on our work's value to others as well as to ourselves.

During World War II, workers were making parachutes by the thousands. The job was tedious, backbreaking, and boring. Each worker hunched over a sewing machine for hours, day after day, with no let-up. The job could have been unbearable. Every morning, though, someone reminded the workers that real, live human beings would use the parachutes they made. Perhaps their husbands, brothers, or sons would use them. The reminder helped.[1]

Perhaps the illustration *is* a little melodramatic. Perhaps it *does* sound like the all-too-familiar management motivational method to manipulate workers to do more better faster. The illustration carries the ring of an important truth. That truth focuses on the word *purpose*.

What purpose does your work have beyond giving you a sense of self-worth and providing a way to earn a living? How does it help somebody else? I hope you can see beyond your work station to the person who eventually will receive value from what you are doing. That person is really depending on you to put something into the product so he or she can get value out of it.

Few jobs provide as dramatic a sense of purpose as, say, being extra-careful so astronauts can fly the shuttle safely or so an airplane will fly safely. But every job contains at least a sliver of a purpose that important. Somebody you may never see will benefit from what you do.

A real estate salesman told an interviewer of the joy he had in helping people find the house they liked. He saw more than a sale and a commission. He saw himself as helping that family find the house which they could live in and turn into a home. No wonder he was successful and respected widely in the medium-sized city in which he lived.

A friend and I were talking about the negatives and positives of our respective jobs as we drank coffee together one morning. He told me how he was dealing with the negatives by focusing on the positives. He's a professor in higher education. He talked about how he had decided to focus more on the students he taught than on the administrative hassles in which he sometimes found himself involved.

At the very moment my friend said those words, a student walked over to our table, almost as if on cue. The student excused himself for interrupting us and then began to tell my friend how much his course from the previous semester had helped him. When the student departed, my friend and I exchanged smiles. His focus on students had benefited both the student and himself. The student had learned, and the professor's level of satisfaction in his job had been raised. The negatives were still there, but the professor was able to deal with them better as he focused on the positives, especially on his relationship of helpfulness to his students.

A traveler tells of seeing in a Japanese church a helpful saying about work. The idea of the Japanese saying was that workers should put the other person's interests into their efforts at work and should try to create something worthwhile for the other person through these efforts.[2]

What real, live, human needs does your job eventually meet? Give some thought to the end product of the job you do. How does it help people?

You may have the privilege of serving people directly—such as in teaching, medicine, social work, plumbing, selling, or a host of other occupations. Then look closely at the needs you are meeting through your work itself. Look, too, at the way you relate to the people with whom you have contact.

Of course, you, like so many, may be a part of a large organization where seeing the end product is more difficult. If so, I encourage you to take two actions.

First, pay attention to the needs of the people with whom you work. Don't be oblivious to their hurts, as if you and your fellow-workers were only unfeeling, inanimate parts of a giant machine. Don't spend your time meddling in other people's lives or gossiping and calling it "showing concern." But do take a genuine interest in other people.

Second, look beyond your individual role to how your work fits into what your business is trying to do. In recent years, basketball fans have been hearing more and more about "role" players. These are team members who go into the game to perform a certain task—like rebound, handle the ball, or guard the other team's best scorer. That player must understand the importance of his or her role in helping the team accomplish its goal of winning the game. So—assuming your job actually is needed!—consider how what you are doing contributes to the overall welfare of your company's work.

For whom are you making "the lights come on"? Give yourself to the task of "making the lights come on" for someone. When you do, you likely will find your joy increased.

Be Thankful: For Activities Besides Work

Work is important, but it is not all-important. Folks sometimes don't get as much joy out of their work as they want because they misunderstand the place of work. We shouldn't expect work to provide us with all the enjoyment we want in our lives. Do you expect your work to give you all the satisfaction you want out of life? If you do, you are doing yourself and your work a disservice. Either your satisfaction level for yourself is too low or your expectations of your job are too high.

The old saying, "Don't put all your eggs in one basket," applies to the matter of joy. Work won't bring us all the joy we want. Indeed, if we expect work to bring us all the joy we want, the joy we get out of work is likely to decrease instead of grow.

Work was never meant to bring us fullness of joy and satisfaction. There *is* more to life than work. Family members are important. Friends are important. Leisure is important. Rest is important. Cultivating a balanced life of personal growth, including spiritual growth, is important. The idea that work is all there is to life just won't work.

If you are unhappy in your job, you may need to back off just a bit. After all, one of the Ten Commandments points out, "Six days shalt thou labor and do all thy work" (Ex. 20:9).

That commandment is still important in a world like ours. The commandment reminds us of the limited value of work and the limited role work should have in our lives.

Cultivate other interests, too. Cultivate the kinds of things that refresh and enhance your life and the lives of others.

Work is important, for all the reasons we've just named and more. Work, though, is not all-important.

If You *Can't* Be Thankful

There's no use kidding about it. I agree with you that some jobs not only seem to be dead-ends; they *are* dead-ends. They *are* routine. In fact, at least some aspects of every job seem meaningless. They seem to benefit no one beyond the next level of management. So, when you run up against that brick wall and your job seems to contain little or no meaning for you or others, I doubt that psyching yourself up to believe the impossible will help very much.

What will help? I have found one thing that does. It's this: *Recognize that these routine, dead-end, meaningless aspects of your job—or even the whole job—do enable you to do at least some things that are truly meaningful.*

My son has become very interested in Japan. In addition to his study of the Japanese language in college here in the United States, he's studied in Japan in a Japanese language institute. Not long ago he took his mother and me to a Japanese restaurant. He suggested that we have sushi as an appetizer.

Sushi, you know, is *raw fish.* I waited with fear and trembling, although I think I projected an image of outward calm and, probably, sophistication. I'm sure I did. I probably looked suave, even.

The sushi arrived. It was wrapped in seaweed and coated with rice. But the seaweed attracted my attention. Somehow I'd never had occasion before that night to thank God for seaweed. I did that evening! ("Thank you, God, for this seaweed Thou hast given us from Thy bounty, wrapped as it is around this piece of raw fish I cannot believe I am about to eat.")

That little vignette from my culinary and family life is intended to illustrate my point. The most difficult, unsatisfying jobs provide something for which we can be thankful if we would but look for it. That something may be only seaweed, but sometimes we have to take what we can get. To cite the most obvious example, people who depend on their jobs only to put bread on their tables, clothes on their backs, and a roof over their heads can be grateful for their work. You've probably heard the old story of the three people someone observed doing construction work. The interviewer asked the workers one by one what they were doing.

The first worker stated, "I'm laying bricks."

The second worker said, "I'm earning a living."

The third worker replied, "I'm building a cathedral."

Almost everyone who tells this story tells it to praise the third worker for being able to see a noble purpose in the work he was doing. And that's fine. Seeing such a purpose is important. Anytime we can find a noble purpose for our lives, let's not pass it up.

There's something to be said for the first worker, too, however. Sooner or later, almost every job degenerates into work. The work may be humdrum, routine, daily. Seeing the purpose may be difficult. However—humdrum, routine, daily, meaningless and all—the work still needs to be done. That's why I think that people deserve praise when they perform the tasks expected of them, even when they always don't understand all of the "why's." Haven't you been in that position enough yourself to agree?

The second worker—the one who said, "I'm earning a living"—deserves praise, too. Working to provide for yourself and your family is not a bad motive for work. In fact, it's a great motive for work. People who work to provide for themselves and others deserve praise.

By the way, one of my mischievous friends tells a perverted sequel to this story. The interviewer came back to the construction site the next day and found only the first two workers. The third worker—the one who said he was building a cathedral—was nowhere in sight.

The interviewer asked, "What happened to the person with that grand and noble purpose? The one who said he was building a cathedral?"

One of the remaining workers said, "Oh, the boss had to let that guy go."

"Had to let him go? Why on earth would anybody in his right mind let a person like that go? A person with such a noble purpose, such a clear vision of what is important in life—why let that kind of person go?" the interviewer inquired.

"Well," the worker replied, "the problem was that he was building a cathedral, just like he said. We're actually supposed to be building a gas station, though."

Give your job the place it deserves!

Personalizing This Idea

When a coworker and I were about to get ready to tackle a task of manual labor, he often would say to me before we got started, "Now, let's take a reading on this." What he meant was, let's survey the situation and get the lay of the land before we start. That way, we'll know more about what we really need to do.

I suggest you do the same concerning your job. What, really, do you think about it? What good, if any, does your work provide for you? for others?

Who is the first person affected within your company organization when you do the job well or poorly? Too, what benefit does your job provide to the ultimate receiver of whatever it is your work is supposed to produce?

Take a reading on those questions. Then go from there to give your job the place it deserves.

Key Points

1. Be thankful: your job helps you.
2. Be thankful: your job helps others.
3. Be thankful: for activities besides work.

Notes

1. Denis Waitley & Reni L. Witt, *The Joy of Working* (New York: Dodd, Mead & Company, 1985), 253.
2. Marsha Sinetar, *Do What You Love, the Money Will Follow* (New York: Paulist Press, 1987), 123.

2
Focus on Reality

Researchers placed a large fish—a pike—and some minnows in an aquarium. The pike had a grand time eating the minnows. After a time, though, the researchers sadistically placed a sheet of glass between the pike and the minnows.

The pike's dinner arrived. He could see the minnows, and he began to try to reach them. Every time he tried, he kept hitting his head on something. He got more and more hungry. He tried harder and harder to get to the minnows. Finally, his head's repeated encounters with the invisible pane of glass got through to his brain. He decided to give up on catching and eating minnows.

Next, these researchers gleefully removed the glass partition. The gutsy minnows, feeling absolutely safe, swam round and round the pike.

What you might think would happen when a hungry, frustrated pike meets tasty minnows did not happen. The pike made no attempt to catch and eat the minnows. Why not? Evidently he was continuing to operate on the perception that he could do nothing to get to the food. He thought he could not catch those minnows if he tried, though they seemed so very near.

All that head-banging had had its effect. The pike just gave up on eating minnows. In fact, he eventually died of starvation in a tank full of food. The food was there, but the pike felt so controlled by outward circumstances that he exerted no effort to satisfy his hunger.[1]

The pike thought he knew where he was. He thought he had assessed his circumstances realistically. Unfortunately for him (or her), he (or she) made decisions on what he *thought* reality was rather than on what reality *actually* was.

In one of the stories from the mythical town of Lake Wobegon, Garrison Keillor observed, "There comes a point where you have to stand up to reality and deny it."[2] People who are unhappy in their jobs tend to do that. They operate on what they *think* is reality and deny the reality that exists. However, if you are not as happy in your job as you think you ought to be, you have arrived at the point where you just *must* try to get as clear a view of reality as possible.

Stop the Blame Game

One of the favorite pastimes of a lot of us is blaming the company or coworkers or somebody else—anybody else—for our lack of happiness, satisfaction, and fulfillment in our jobs. We play the "blame game." We let ourselves believe that all our unhappiness is someone else's fault.

This notion started in the Garden of Eden when Adam blamed Eve for his problem. And it hasn't ended. Most of us are experts at blaming others. To make a bad matter worse, we then label that perspective "reality."

When we operate on the basis of that view of reality, we blame our unhappiness and lack of fulfillment in our jobs on:

• *The way we're supervised.* "My boss (or his boss or her boss or the big boss) is a dummy, a tyrant, a climber, or a crook (or all the preceding)."

• *Company policy.* "Did you ever see so many meaningless rules? And what about the paperwork? We can't do anything. There's no room for creativity."

● *Working conditions.* "We're always just snowed under with work, and they don't care. And, have you seen that place we have to work? They call it an office. Nobody should have to work in that kind of place."

● *Interpersonal relationships.* "There's so much back-biting. Most of these sharks I work with would turn on their own grandmothers to get ahead."

● *Salary and the lack thereof.* "I'm worth a heckuva lot more than they're paying me. And besides, I know folks who don't do half as much as I do and they get paid more."

You may be saying, "Yeah, that's right. That's what's bugging me." I would not disagree with you that all of these matters are frustrating problems. They frustrate many of us. In fact, these problems are the major categories that show up on employee surveys about what makes them unhappy with their jobs.[3]

Now that we have identified the things that make us unhappy in our work, where does that leave us, except angry and frustrated? When we merely have identified the problems that make us unhappy, we have only shown ourselves to be experts at playing the "blame game." We've not solved the problem. Focusing on reality calls for more than merely analyzing the problem and finding someone to blame it on. Focusing on reality calls for coming up with the solution.

Don't fix the blame—on upline management, on your co-workers, on the weather, on interruptions, on whatever. Fix the problem—as much as *you* can.

Take Control of What You *Can* Control

Let's put aside for the moment the possibility that you might be able to change any of the frustrating problems in the list in the preceding section. Let's just assume that you don't have a prayer of a chance of bringing about changes in company policy, your salary, the way your co-workers act, the working conditions, and certainly not the company CEO and all those between you and him. In fact, that assumption may well be reality in many if not most work situations. At least, you are setting yourself up for a life of misery if you base your happiness in your job on your ability—or the ability of others—to change those conditions. Then what do you need to do about your job unhappiness?

One motivation expert has identified the stages of problem-solving as follows. We first tend to ignore the problem, hoping it will go away. Next we try to deny there is a problem. Then we "progress" to the stage of blaming the problem on someone or something else.

We will solve the problem only if we move to the fourth stage. At that stage, we assume responsibility for solving the problem—at least for solving our part of the problem. This stage is a prelude to the final stage, that of finding a solution.[4]

I hope you are ready to move from the "blame others" stage to the "assume responsibility" stage. To find greater joy in our jobs, we need to *focus on what we can control* and assume responsibility for that.

So much of many, if not most, jobs is like weather to a farmer. The farmer can't control the weather. If it rains too much or too little, it just rains too much or too little. The farmer can't stop or start the rain.

What's the answer for the farmer? Should he spend his days and nights uttering curses against the clouds or the clear skies? About the only good that would do would be to release the tensions within the farmer. That's about all complaining about the company "system" does, too. It may make us feel better for a brief time, but the problem will still be there.

What must the farmer do? He has to take what comes and make the best of it. He can use the weather to his advantage sometimes by adjusting to it, reacting positively to it. He must recognize that he just can't control some things, like the weather. He *can* control his reaction to these things, however. He can make plans to work with the weather as much as possible, rather than against it.

So, the farmer exercises control over those areas over which he has control. Those areas may not be many or large, but he works with what he has to work with.

Thus, for example, suppose you have a problem with company policy. You can't change the policy. The decision has been made. What are your choices?

(1) You could simply go along unhappily, railing against the stupidity of the situation. That's understandable as a first reaction, but it's unhealthy and unproductive when that's all one does.

(2) You could ignore or counteract company policy. Such a choice might lead to rather nasty consequences, depending on the importance of the policy and the flagrancy of the violation.

(3) You could go to another company. This solution certainly is a viable alternative. Intolerable company policies sometimes press people so tightly that this action seems to be the only one they can take. Let's not kid ourselves about the new company, though. Do you think the new company won't have policies? You might like the policies of the new company better than those of the previous company. Likely, you still will have to deal with policies that don't quite fit your preferences.

(4) Another possible action is to adjust to the demands. That is, find opportunities for happiness within or alongside these demands. Perhaps, when the reasons for the policy become clearer, the policy itself might even become more acceptable. Or, you may need simply to accept that this policy is the way it is. You then would need to find other areas—areas over which you have control—for happiness.

The strength of the fourth choice is that you are acting rather than simply reacting. You are seeking ways to react positively to a situation with which you do not agree and that is not of your own making.

Attitude is tremendously important in dealing with life. Famed social scientist Dr. Ashley Montagu tells of interviewing two young men who had survived the horrors of World War II, including two years in prison at Auschwitz. When the young men were released, they found that all of their families had been put to death. The two young men made their way to the United States, where they entered medical school. There they met Dr. Montagu.

Dr. Montagu was impressed that in spite of all they had been through, they seemed to be cheerful human beings. He asked them what had enabled them to overcome the tragic experiences they had suffered. They said that they and a group of other people had simply decided that whatever happened to them short of death, they would not allow it to get them down. They would survive. So they tried to be as cheerful as they could under the weight of the circumstances. They maintained a positive view of themselves, not allowing themselves to feel inferior to the enemies who had imprisoned them.[5]

Hugh Downs, popular television personality for many years, said that a turning point in his life came when he was twenty-three years old. He suddenly realized that he, not someone else, was totally responsible for his own actions.[6] What does this idea mean toward the goal of getting more happiness out of a job you sometimes can't stand? It means that while enjoyment may not be in the job situation itself, enjoyment *does* relate to how one *reacts* to the job situation.

Not long ago, a magazine editor I work with received an unusual letter. The writer *insisted* that the editor publish his letter. The letter called readers to stand up and be counted about many matters the writer considered to be wrong. It's time to be courageous, the writer exhorted. It's time to stand up and be counted, regardless of the consequences, the letter continued.

When the editor made it to the end of the diatribe, he discovered the writer who wanted everyone to stand up and be counted had requested that his name not be used. In fact, this person of such great courage had signed his name, "Anonymous."

So you're not as happy in your job as you wish you were. It's time to take your share of the responsibility for the happiness. You'll spend perhaps a third of your adult life actually on the job at your place of work. Enjoying that time is too important for you to stand around and wait for other people—even a company—to make you happy.

Wait a minute, some of you may be saying. *Are you suggesting I should just take whatever comes and keep my mouth shut like a good little girl or boy?*

Nope, that's not what I'm suggesting. There's a place for making your feelings known. There's a place for letting management know when and where the shoe is pinching tightly or whether we even *have* shoes. There's also a place for blowing off steam with fellow employees. We need to beware, though, of the unhealthy nature of those "pity parties" that go on and on, day after day, week in and week out, covering the same subjects.

Are you seeking ways to increase your enjoyment of a job you just can't stand sometimes? Then, don't hitch your happiness wagon to a ball of mud but to a star! Take control of what you *can* control.

A few years ago, Studs Terkel, a best-selling author, set out to listen to what the working people of the United States were saying about their work and how they felt about it. What the people said revealed a great deal of dissatisfaction with their jobs.

The writer also found, however, what he called "the happy few who find a savor in their daily job."[7] Reflecting, he asked, "But don't these satisfactions . . . tell us more about the person than about his task? Perhaps."[8] Your—and my—desire for more happiness in our jobs reveals something about our jobs *and* about ourselves.

As Walter Anderson, editor of *Parade* magazine, summarized, "Three factors determine who we are. Heredity, environment and, most important, our response to both."[9] You can't control a good bit of what happens to you in your job, but you can control how you react to what happens. A lot of this book is aimed at helping you identify those areas you can control and get on with the business of doing something about it. A good bit of whatever happiness you gain in your work will be a do-it-yourself job.

In his book *A Touch of Wonder*, Arthur Gordon told of an experience in World War II that taught him a great deal about the importance of the way one looks at life. Gordon described the winter of 1942-43 as "the bleakest period of my life so far."[10] The cold, wet weather and the general miserableness of the entire situation demoralized almost everybody.

One sergeant, though, somehow maintained a continually cheerful attitude. Gordon watched him whistling with joy as the sergeant labored to free an airplane that was almost buried in the mud after having run off the runway.

Gordon sarcastically asked the sergeant how he could whistle in such a dismal situation. The sergeant grinned and replied, "'When the facts won't budge, you have to bend your attitudes to fit them, that's all.'"[11]

The sergeant was right on target. If you are skeptical about how such positive thinking can help you deal with your problems, I encourage you to give it a chance. *What* we allow, even encourage, ourselves to think about and *how* we think about it *does* affect reality.

In fact, we actually deal with reality *as we perceive it*, not as it really is. Of course, we are healthiest when our perception of reality squares most closely with reality itself. Our knowledge always is partial and distorted to a greater or lesser extent.

Business consultant Karl Albrecht points out that an unhappy person fails to grasp that positives and negatives, successes and failures, are one's evaluations of reality. They are not reality itself.[12]

Of course, the particular piece of reality in question may truly be a negative. What shall we do? As the sergeant did, we may need to bend our attitudes to fit the facts. Why should we live unhappily if we can deal most constructively with the same facts with an attitude of happiness? Attitude toward the facts is one major element of life over which we *do* have control. Abraham Lincoln said that most people are about as happy as they make up their minds to be.

Focus on What *Really* Provides Job Satisfaction

What really provides job satisfaction? Research studies have revealed a surprising answer. What makes people happy in their jobs is *not* simply the reverse of what makes them happy.[13] That idea sounded like doubletalk to me the first time I ran onto it. The research findings have been verified over and over for the past thirty years, however.

The kinds of things that make people dissatisfied with their jobs are the matters we dealt with earlier in this chapter—supervision, company policy, working conditions, interpersonal relations, and salary, plus status, job security, and events in one's personal life.[14] A person might think that having these matters dealt with positively would bring about happiness. That is, if your supervisor and all his supervisors were great, then you would be a happy employee. And, if company policy were totally fixed right, that, too, would bring happiness to you as an employee. And if working conditions and interpersonal relationships were all they should be, then you would be happy. And if your salary were what it ought to be, happiness would be yours. And so on.

Sounds logical, doesn't it? Sounded logical to me, too.

That's not what the research has shown, though. If a worker had all of those matters taken care of, he still would not necessarily be happy. He just wouldn't be *unhappy*. All of these matters are important in preventing *dissatisfaction*. These matters, though, don't provide *satisfaction*.

Please stay with me. This concept is important. It may even be the most important concept you need to grasp about job satisfaction.

So, if all those things I just named don't provide job satisfaction, what will? What is required for true job *satisfaction*, true happiness in one's job? These are the things that workers themselves said provided real joy in their jobs: achievement, recognition for achievement, the work itself, responsibility, advancement, and the possibility of growth.[15]

How do these elements of job satisfaction strike you? Do they fit with your experience? Let me tell you how Herzberg and other researchers did their work. Then you test your own experience.

Herzberg and his associates simply asked workers to recall events in their jobs that resulted either in marked job satisfaction or dissatisfaction.[16] This same study has been repeated with various kinds of workers. The results have been basically the same. The kinds of things that make us happy and unhappy with our jobs respectively are on different lists.

Notice the kinds of things that brought job satisfaction —achievement, recognition for achievement, the work itself, responsibility, advancement, and the possibility of growth. Obviously, the company has responsibilities for providing a situation in which employees can experience these elements in job satisfaction. As one of the workers Studs Terkel interviewed said, " 'I think most of us are looking for a calling, not a job. Most of us, like the assembly line worker, have jobs that are too small for our spirit. Jobs are not big enough for people.' "[17] Companies need to make jobs big enough for the human spirit.

The company does not bear the full responsibility, of course. The individual worker bears responsibility, too. At least a part of what this idea suggests is that we must not expect such matters as company policy, supervisors, or even salary to make us happy—at least not for very long. Genuine job satisfaction comes from other sources. Genuine job satisfaction comes from such factors as achievement, a sense of pride in the work itself, and exercising the opportunity to grow.

The company is responsible for providing an environment where these factors can flourish. Whether the company does a good job or a poor one in providing such a situation, though, we need to take some initiative in these areas if we are serious about getting more joy out of our work. If we are going to get much happiness out of some jobs, we are going to have to make up in our attitudes and actions what the company does not provide.

A heavy equipment operator told Studs Terkel, "'You drive down the road and you say, "I worked on this road." If there's a bridge, you say, "I worked on this bridge." Or you drive by a building and you say, "I worked on this building." Maybe it don't mean anything to anybody else, but there's a certain amount of pride knowing you did your bit."'[18] Stupid company policies and dumb management actions can't take that sense of pride away.

Personalizing This Idea

A worker's first day on the job went great. His job was to paint the white line down the middle of the highway. The company was the low bidder, and this was a low-budget operation. The boss had given the new worker a paint brush and a can full of white paint. The boss had instructed the worker in how to do the job. He was to go to the middle of the road, set down the paint can, paint a white stripe ten steps long, skip five steps, and paint another white stripe.

The worker's very first day, he painted ten miles of white stripes. The boss was absolutely amazed. The next day, the worker painted five miles of white stripes. Not bad, but the boss was a little concerned.

The third day was worse. The worker painted only a quarter-mile of white stripes. The boss was greatly troubled. The employee's productivity was going down instead of up. So the boss decided to have a talk with this once-promising employee.

The boss and the employee sat down for a talk. The boss said, "Let me check up on what you're doing. Your first day you painted ten miles of white lines. I was not only pleased; I was amazed. The second day, though, you painted only five miles, and today you painted only a quarter-mile. What gives? Let's talk about how you are going about doing your work. Let me ask you some questions.

"Are you going to the middle of the road?"

"Yes," the worker said.

"Are you setting the paint can down?"

"Yes, I'm doing that."

"Are you painting a white stripe ten steps long?"

"Yes."

"And then are you leaving five steps free of paint?"

"Yes."

"Are you then repeating the process all day long?"

"Yes."

"Well," the boss said, "I'm puzzled. What do you suppose is causing you to paint fewer and fewer white stripes every day?"

The employee pondered the question a moment and then said, "I think I know. I think it's because I have to spend so much time walking back to the paint can."

Obviously, this person did not have a realistic assessment of the situation! What about you? How far is it to *your* paint can? How close to reality is your perspective on your job? Are you, like the pike and the painter, operating on an unrealistic view of your situation?

Are you blaming your lack of satisfaction in your job solely on external hindrances? What actions could you take in those areas where you yourself have control that would help you squeeze more happiness out of a job you sometimes—maybe even most of the time—can't stand? What do you think it would really take to make you happy in your job? How can you get to there from where you are now?

Key Points

1. Stop the blame game.
2. Take control of what you *can* control.
3. Focus on what really provides job satisfaction.

Notes

1. Paul Hersey and Kenneth Blanchard, *Management of Organizational Behavior*, 2nd ed. (Englewood Cliffs, N. J.: Prentice-Hall, Inc., 1972), 20.

2. Garrison Keillor, *Leaving Home* (New York: Viking Penguin Inc., 1987), 40.

3. Frederick Herzberg, *Work and the Nature of Man* (Cleveland: The World Publishing Company, 1966), 74.

4. Andrew S. Grove, *High Output Management* (New York: Random House, 1983), 194.

5. Dennis Wholey, *Discovering Happiness: Personal Conversations About Getting the Most Out of Life* (New York: Avon Books, 1986), 260-261.

6. Patrice D. Horn, "Twenty Years of Growing Up," *Psychology Today* (May 1987), 24.

7. Studs Terkel, *Working: People Talk About What They Do All Day*

and How They Feel About What They Do (New York: Pantheon Books, 1974), xi.

8. Ibid.

9. Walter Anderson, *Courage Is a Three-Letter Word* (New York: Fawcett Crest, 1986), 25.

10. Arthur Gordon, *A Touch of Wonder* (Old Tappan, N. J.: Fleming H. Revell Company, 1974), 196.

11. Ibid., 197.

12. Karl Albrecht, *Brain Power: Learn to Improve Your Thinking Skills* (Englewood Cliffs, N. J.: Prentice-Hall, Inc., 1980), 116.

13. Herzberg, *Work and the Nature of Man*, 76.

14. Ibid., 95-96.

15. Ibid.

16. Ibid., 71.

17. Terkel, *Working*, xxiv.

18. Ibid., 26.

3
Think Creatively About Your Job

Consider this statement: *There are three misteaks in this sentance.* What mistakes can you find? (If you're an expert on English style, please ignore the "there are." I know that "there are" is a weak way with which to begin a sentence. OK?)

Back to the statement. If you're a pretty fair speller, you probably recognized immediately that the word "misteaks" should be spelled "mistakes." You also realized that the word "sentance" should be spelled "sentence."

Maybe you also caught what I missed the first time a friend showed this to me. Since I found the two spelling mistakes almost immediately, my brain evidently thought that looking for another spelling mistake would be a pretty good idea. So that's the kind of mistake I zeroed in on. But I couldn't find a third spelling mistake. Finally I gave up. I could not find the third mistake. Did you?

The third mistake is the word "three." There really are only *two*, not three, mistakes in the statement. I missed the third one because my brain became rather proud of itself for having spotted the two spelling mistakes so quickly. My brain assumed that since the first two mistakes were spelling mistakes, any other mistakes were spelling mistakes, too. Good reasoning, but my brain was wrong.

Our brains are marvelous instruments. They process a lot of information in a split second. One way by which the brain processes the vast amount of information it receives is by developing mental routines, standard ways of dealing with what it considers routine information. It processes this information automatically, fitting it into preset categories. Thus, certain thought patterns become grooved into particular channels.[1] This technique is quite useful on most occasions, but it can also lead to the wrong conclusions.

That was the case with my brain's erroneous logic about the mistakes in the sentence. My brain got into a groove and was reluctant to look for any possibilities outside that groove.

I hope this mental exercise has shown how easily we can let ourselves think in routine ways about even the simplest matters. When we do, we run the risk of missing valuable information and coming to erroneous conclusions.

What does all of this have to do with finding ways to be happier in the jobs we sometimes can't stand? A good bit, I think. We can and do miss valuable information and thus come to erroneous conclusions about our jobs. We can think in grooves about our jobs as with everything else. What specifically does this mean for you, then? This: it's possible that you've thought a certain way about your job for so long that you've got ruts in your brain, like gullies formed by rain on a hillside! Getting out of such ruts won't be easy. But, learning to think creatively about your job is an important step toward being happier in it.

I'm going to make three big suggestions in this chapter about how you can think creatively about your job. I want you to put these suggestions into practice for the benefit they offer to *you*, not to your employer. If your employer accidentally receives positive results from your putting these suggestions into practice, well and good. It won't hurt and most likely will help. I urge you, though, to think about these suggestions *first* for their benefit to you.

Master the Basics of Your Job

One of the natural tendencies we human beings seem to have when we find ourselves in an unhappy job situation is to begin to slough off and give less than our best. Our reasoning appears perfectly logical to us. Unfortunately for us, though, we are missing some important data and are headed for an unproductive conclusion.

Imagine a person's brain processing information about an unhappy job situation: "My work is boring and unrewarding. My bosses don't appreciate me and my work. They don't pay me enough for what I do. They don't free me up to do what I can really do. Therefore, since I have to have this job, or at least until I can find another one, I'll show them. I'll do the least I can do to get by. Why should I break my neck when they don't appreciate me?"

Let's say that the data in that paragraph is correct as far as it goes. Let's say that the job indeed is boring and unrewarding, that the pay is too low, that the employee does not receive signals that he or she is appreciated, and that unreasonable restrictions do exist. Still, the brain of this person has processed the data in such a way as to result in at least two erroneous conclusions.

The first wrong conclusion is that revenge somehow will accomplish a positive result. After all, "showing them" *is* revenge. Does the person expect to be rewarded for revenge? That's crazy logic, but the reaction is common.

The second erroneous conclusion is that sloughing off on one's work will lead to job satisfaction. Don't you recall from the previous chapter that job satisfaction comes from things like achievement and growth?

Consider also a sad by-product of the brain's erroneous conclusions. Something in most people called a conscience makes them believe that they ought to give a fair day's work for a fair day's pay. When they *don't* give an honest day's work, even when they reason they are not being treated fairly themselves, most people feel that something about the whole deal is not morally right. So, when they slough off, they add at least a little bit of guilt to their already unhappy lives. Not good, right?

Therefore, people who are not as happy in their jobs as they want to be need to check their thinking and give fresh, creative thought to their jobs. When they do, they might well find that they are operating on some erroneous mental routines that have been grooved into their brains. They need to climb out of their ruts and explore some new ways of thinking about their jobs.

Since happiness in our jobs really comes from our positive attainments and our recognition for these attainments, accurate thinking that takes all the data into account leads to an important conclusion. It's this: Taking positive action to show mastery of at least the basics of our jobs is a must for increasing our happiness in those jobs.

This conclusion makes sense when we give clear thought to the matter. After all, why should we not want to take those actions that will lead to the goal we truly want to reach—greater happiness in our work? What sort of perverted logic leads us to think otherwise? As motivational writers Denis Waitley and Reni L. Witt say, "Enjoyment comes from doing our best. At our best, we want to do and be our best, even when the work we are doing is not our first choice and does not give us the joy we want. . . . Having pride in one's work . . . brings lasting joy."[2]

Thus, you will help yourself to greater happiness in your job if you will throw yourself wholeheartedly into the task of mastering it. Find out all that your job requires. If you think you haven't received adequate training for your job, ask for help. Take every opportunity to learn on your own. Then, absolutely do all that your job requires of you. If people were as creative in mastering their jobs as they are at finding ways to slough off without getting caught, they would be a lot happier.

Let's say that you do master your job but no one—not even your supervisor—shows appreciation for what you do. I know at least a little about how you will feel. Obviously, appreciation from others is important. We all feel that way. We all need to know we are appreciated. Like drought-parched grass responding to a summer shower, most of us thrive on the smallest show of appreciation.

People being what they are, however, your boss(es) may not notice. You may have to praise yourself. If so, do so—and heartily! In fact, folks who have mastered their jobs deserve to praise themselves even if no one else does it.

Don't break your arm patting yourself on the back, but *do* pat yourself on the back. It's good for you, and it will give you such a feeling of accomplishment! And that's not bad. At a healthy level, this feeling is called self-esteem. I like what Pierce Walker, a farmer, said about himself and his work, "If you weren't proud of your work, you wouldn't have no place on the farm. 'Cause you don't work by the hour. And you put in a lot of hours, I tell ya. You wouldn't stay out here till dark and after if you were punchin' a clock. If you didn't like your work and have pride in it, you wouldn't do that."[3]

So, as you master your work, be proud. It's okay to be proud when you've done your best, even if no one else shows appreciation—make that *especially if no one else shows appreciation*. In fact, as the advertisements are telling us, it's the right thing to do.

Thus, the first big suggestion for thinking creatively about your job is that you must take steps to *show mastery of the basics of your job*. Here's the second: *go beyond the basics*.

Go Beyond the Basics

Before the time of Columbus, the motto of the nation of Spain was "nothing more beyond." The name reflected the nation's geographical location at the remote edge of the world—the known world, that is. Likely the motto "nothing more beyond" also reflected a bit of national pride. Spain felt it was at the pinnacle of success.

A funny thing happened about that time, however. Columbus sailed the ocean blue and in 1492 found that there was a whole lot more beyond what could be seen from the shores of Spain. The world-changing discoveries of Columbus led Spain to change its motto from "nothing more beyond" to "more beyond."

When you have mastered the basics of your job, look for the "more beyond." Are there creative ways of doing your work? Could it possibly be that *you* could find ways to improve how you do your work? Could *you* find ways that would save time and energy, ways that would save money for the company, ways that would add quality to the product?

Many times, of course, what appears to be a better way is a way that has already been tried and found wanting. You need to be aware of that reality before you plunge headlong into what only *appears* to be a better way. Your "better way" may foul things up, unless you check it out carefully. Nobody is fond of a fellow who exuberantly announces that he has invented a wonderful, labor-saving device—and then from behind the curtain he shoves a square something-or-other that he calls a wheel.

The fact remains, though, that the best ways of doing most things probably haven't been discovered. Mastery of your present job will give you the insight and experience needed for finding improved ways of performing the task and producing whatever it is that you produce. When you have become an expert on the basics of your job, you probably will know as much about that job as anyone, even your supervisor. (Maybe even *especially* your supervisor.) Who else is in a better position to make improvements than you?

The company for which I work produces educational materials. One such product consists of a large envelope filled with posters, worksheets, maps, and other such items. Teachers use these materials in teaching their classes. Perhaps forty or more pieces of paper are in each envelope. Although many appreciative people use this product successfully and praise it accordingly, one feature of the product has received many complaints from teachers over the years. The various pieces of paper are packaged in random order rather than in order of use. So, the teachers must put the items in order themselves.

No way of correcting the problem could be found without costing money and thus calling for an increase in the price charged the customer. Or so it was thought.

When customers continued to complain, the people who printed and assembled the materials took another look. Lo and behold—there was another way! Someone saw it.

Maybe you could do the same sort of thing. Keep a creative eye out as you do your work. You may be able to find at least one improvement you can make in the process or the product.

Don't stifle your creativity just because your job satisfaction is not at an acceptable level. That's the time to turn on the creativity and go beyond where you are now. Even if no one else recognizes your accomplishment, you will have the satisfaction within yourself of having done a good job—even a creative job. If someone recognizes what you've done and praises you for it, so much the better.

Several friends and I were enjoying a meal together at a good restaurant—not expensive, but nice enough. The restaurant was quite busy. Our waitress was quite busy herself.

She was especially attentive, courteous, and helpful to us, in spite of the fact that she was busy serving many tables other than our own.

Okay, I admit it: she *was* attractive! But, and I am really and truly being honest, her efficiency and helpfulness impressed us even more. She moved from one table to another with ease. She returned to our table often, checking on our wants and needs. She never let our coffee cups get empty. Her work was special, and the four of us at the table talked about her excellent service. Then, when she came by our table to serve us some more coffee, one of us remarked to her about our observation of, and appreciation for, her effectiveness, helpfulness, and efficiency. (It never hurts to compliment good work.) We marveled at how she could do such a good job when she had so many tables to wait on. She replied, "It's easy. You've just got to have a plan."

She had done the kind of creative thinking about her work that enabled her to make the most of her ability and opportunity. Not only had she mastered the basics of being a good waitress, but also she had gone beyond the basics and found the most effective and helpful ways of doing her job. She gave the impression that she got a good bit of joy out of her job, too. She's an example of the pay-off that comes from thinking creatively about one's job.

Adapt to Changing Circumstances

We'd do well to act more like flies rather than bees as we approach our jobs. Place bees in a bottle, leave the top open, lay it on its side with the end toward a light, and the bees will fly to the light. They zero in on the light; they think of nothing else as they try to get out. Thus, they ignore the open end through which they could gain their freedom if they would but think creatively about their situation.

What about the flies? Place them in a bottle, leave the top open, lay the bottle on its side with the end toward a light, and the flies become very innovative. Instead of locking in on the light, the flies will move helter-skelter around the inside of the bottle. In a short time, their creative activity will enable them to escape.[4]

Are you more like a trapped bee than an innovative fly? You need to learn to adapt yourself in the way you look at your job and the way you act in it. To get trapped in the mode of resentment, defeatism, and unhappiness is to be imprisoned by yourself. Such a situation calls for exploring the options rather than locking in to a certain pattern.

More than one person has become increasingly, perhaps unbearably, unhappy on his job because he did not adapt to the changing circumstances and demands of that job. Perhaps it was computers, new processes, or new management. Whatever the case, he failed to adapt to changed conditions. Maybe he *couldn't* adapt. Or maybe he *wouldn't*, thinking the effort wasn't worth it.

Remember, though, that all of life changes. Why should we expect our jobs to remain static? Well, the answer of course is that we shouldn't. Our jobs don't remain static; they change. So must we. To be happier on our jobs, we must adapt creatively to the changing circumstances we inevitably will face.

Personalizing This Idea

A mathematician found himself having to travel by air a great deal in connection with his work. He worried that a bomb might be placed on the airplane in which he was traveling. In fact, he calculated that the chances were one in a hundred thousand—make that a million (I fly fairly often, and I feel better about the higher odds)—that a bomb would be on the plane. He considered one in a million to be a rather high risk. Thus, every time he was scheduled to go on a trip, he just could not convince himself to get on the airplane.

As his work suffered from his unwillingness to fly, he sought frantically for a solution. Then a creative flash struck like a bolt of lightning. "It's true," he reasoned, "that the chances are one in a million that a bomb will be on any airplane I fly. But the chances of there being not one but *two* bombs on board are one in *two* million."

This creative thought comforted the mathematician. From them on he flew with no trace of anxiety. He simply packed a bomb in his own suitcase whenever he traveled!

You, too, can think creatively about your job. I hope, though, you will do it with more insight than did the mathematician.

Have you mastered the basics of your job? Are you demonstrating that mastery?

What aspects of your job could you improve on? Take some time to think about all the elements of your job. Why are you doing them in the way you are doing them? Are there one or more parts to the process for which you are responsible that don't seem to make sense you? Can you identify any shortcuts that would still achieve—and even go beyond—the quality goals expected of you and not cause difficulty for a coworker? Could you make improvements that would benefit your company and ultimately the customer?

Give these questions some creative thought. And, remember, think about them for yourself and your own happiness. Think about them for your own benefit. When you're asking these questions, give yourself permission to look out for your own self-interest. If you're not as happy in your job as you want to be, it makes sense to think about your job in ways that would stand the greatest chance of bringing positive results—to *you* first, and only secondarily to your employer. You can increase your happiness in the job you sometimes can't stand by thinking creatively about your approach to the job.

Business writers Denis Waitley and Reni Witt suggest,

"The happiest people in the world are those who are working up to their potential."[5] You may think you are not able to live up to your potential in your present job, but the closer you can get to this goal, the happier you will be. Creative, innovative thinking about your job can increase your chances of moving toward that goal.

Key Points

1. Master the basics of your job.
2. Go beyond the basics.
3. Adapt to changing circumstances.

Notes

1. Karl Albrecht, *Brain Power: Learn to Improve Your Thinking Skills* (Englewood Cliffs, N. J.: Prentice-Hall, Inc., 1980), 34.

2. Denis Waitley & Reni L. Witt, *The Joy of Working* (New York: Dodd, Mead & Company, 1985), 213.

3. Studs Terkel, *Working: People Talk About What They Do All Day and How They Feel About What They Do* (New York: Pantheon Books, 1974), 6.

4. Waitley & Witt, *The Joy of Working,* 119-120.

5. Ibid., 93.

4
Build Positive Relationships

A little boy came home from school with an unhappy expression on his face. Obviously, the day had not gone well. His mother expressed her concern, inquiring, "I have the feeling things didn't go too well for you today. What's the matter?" The little boy replied, "I'm the only one I know at school."

Lots of Americans evidently feel like that little boy. A recent Gallup poll revealed that as many as four out of ten Americans feel lonely, frequently or occasionally. Analysis of the data led to the conclusion that Americans are the loneliest people in the world.[1]

This conclusion seems logical when we consider how most Americans live. Many of us live in air-conditioned houses, shut off from other people by closed windows and locked doors. We travel to work in automobiles, often alone. Or we use public transportation, again isolating ourselves by gazing out the window, reading, or listening to a radio or a tape by earphones. Even when we are with people, we often are actually alone.

The situation at work for many is not much different. We do our work *beside*, not necessarily *with*, others. We fulfill our role, they fulfill their roles, and we all seem at times to behave like mere cogs in a giant machine. No wonder so many of us are lonely. We live like robots.

An important ingredient that leads to happiness in almost any situation, and certainly at work, is the quality of our relationships with other people. Indeed, employees at an assembly-line in Tennessee identified relating to other people as one of the most important aspects of their work. And, employees in Massachusetts who worked at home on computer terminals said they wanted to be able to bring their children to a child-care center and work together with fellow employees. The reason? They wanted to be able to talk to one another rather than to work in isolation.[2] Therefore, consider how you can build positive relationships with the people in your workplace and thus increase your own chances for happiness there.

Relating to Fellow Employees

Whom do you know at work? Can you name at least one person in the family of the person who works nearest to you? What do you know about your nearest coworker? Where is he or she from, originally? And, beyond surface information, what are that person's goals, dreams, concerns, and hurts? Are you friends? Are you even acquaintances to one degree or another? At the most basic level of relationship required for productive work, do you even work cooperatively with that person?

What is the potential for your developing positive relationships with your coworkers? A lot? A little? Not much? None? Maybe there are good reasons for any distance that may exist between you and the folks with whom you work. After all, working with other people on a task does not necessarily mean they are the people to whom you would choose to reveal your deepest feelings—or even your not-so-deep feelings. You may or may not be compatible with your coworkers. The best you may be able to achieve is a cordial, cooperative, though distant relationship with your coworkers. But enhancing your relationships with them, to whatever degree, *can* be an important, even indispensable, ingredient in achieving the happiness you desire at work.

One writer in the field of helping people get more joy out of their work suggests that building social relationships among a small group of people at work is one way an employee can create a more enjoyable work environment.[3] From both observation and personal experience, I believe the idea is correct.

I'm a member of an informal lunch-table organization at my place of employment. It's affectionately called "Table A." At this revered table, we discuss and decide all manner of issues—large, small, and in-between. No topic is too sublime or too ridiculous for this noble group. We middle-aged (it's the truth that hurts) members of Table A schedule an annual picnic and have just established another annual occasion—the Annual Groundhog Day Pizza Pig-out.

A bond of acceptance unites the members of Table A. The friendships formed and demonstrated among the group that frequents Table A go a long way toward providing a measure of happiness in the jobs each of us performs.

A friend of mine from earlier days served in the United States Army during World War II. He was a part of a unit that was in the thick of the fighting in Europe. Along with the rest of his unit, he often found himself in difficult and dangerous circumstances—an unpleasant job to say the least.

Guess who some of his dearest friends are now. You're right: the members of that unit. The men are now scattered over the United States, but they will travel hundreds of miles to get together for a reunion. Distance does not matter. Something about their mutual experiences during the war welded these men together with an unbreakable bond.

When the unit was first formed in World War II, the young men had little in common. They came from different parts of the country, held different values, and had varied skills. But the shared experience of war drew them strongly together and brought them a measure of joy under exceedingly difficult circumstances.

The experience of my friend has a degree of application to the workplace. Only in the rarest of instances are people in the ordinary workplace involved in truly life-and-death issues. Still, the quality of our relationships with one another can add to or detract from our sense of happiness in our jobs.

How, then, can we build positive relationships with coworkers? Let me suggest these seven answers:

1. Emphasize Cooperation Instead of Competitiveness

Consider this experiment. Say you approach two boys, give them each an end of a rope with a knot in the middle, draw a line between the two boys, and tell them you will give each of them a nickel each time the knot crosses that line. What will the boys do? Likely they will engage in a tug-of-war. The result will be that one boy will be a winner and the other a loser each time they struggle with the rope.[4]

Is that the only option? What if the two boys decided to cooperate instead of compete? Without breaking any rules, the two boys could saw the knot back and forth across the line you have drawn. The result would be many more nickels for each of them. Plus, both would be winners.

I'm not denying that competition exists in the workplace for such things as promotions, affirmation, and perhaps even salary increases. Emphasizing cooperation more and competition less would help all of us and likely even the work itself.

A feeling of being threatened is a distinct barrier to friendship. If you want to build a friendship, remove the barrier. Approach your coworkers as one who wishes to cooperate more than as one who wishes to compete.

2. Learn to Care About Others

A second step toward building positive relationships with coworkers is to express interest in them. This favorite quotation speaks volumes: "Let us be kind to one another, for most of us are fighting a hard battle."[5] We need to increase our sensitivity to others' hurts and learn to care about them.

We would probably be surprised to learn the difficulties through which some of our coworkers have traveled in the past and may be living in even now. Those difficulties likely affect their workplace behavior. I've noticed that quite often the person who is most obnoxious is the person who is carrying around a hurt that has not healed. The hurt may go back even to childhood days.

Expressing care and concern for coworkers opens the door of friendship in many cases. When one employee expresses concern for another as a human being, the workplace becomes more than a giant machine. It becomes a place where people's humanity is recognized and thus where a measure of joy becomes possible. (Too, studies have shown that productivity is greater when the focus is on the human needs of employees rather than on productivity itself.[6])

3. Accept the Uniqueness of Other People

Years ago, Art Linkletter hosted a daytime television show called "People Are Funny." The show no longer exists, but people are still funny. All of us are a little funny, in fact. That is, we are all unique—some more than others, of course! We'll help ourselves in building positive relationships with coworkers if we will simply acknowledge people's uniqueness and be prepared to accept other people for who they are.

If you've ever ridden the subway in New York City, you're aware that the subway walls are where many people have tried to leave behind something by which to be remembered. Graffiti artists have covered the walls with various sorts of mementoes and messages.

A visitor to New York City tells of seeing on an advertising poster in the subway a picture of a very proper older gentleman. To this picture someone had added a cartoon-type balloon and had scrawled what perhaps was intended to be a racy comment. The words in the balloon had the older gentleman saying, "I like grils."

Underneath that unintelligible statement someone had written a correction, "It's girls, stupid, not grils." In still another hand, though, this third message appeared: "But what about us grils?"[7]

Too many folks subscribe to this saying the Hungarians have: "Outside Hungary, no life you'll find. And if you do, it's not our kind."[8] This little piece of verse is no reflection on the Hungarians, though. Substitute in that statement whatever country, state, group, or characteristic you value. You will find the statement applies. We all tend to want to accept only those people who are most like us. We'll do well, though, to broaden our acceptance of other people. Doing so is a must for building positive relationships.

4. Be Generous with Affirmation

Honest praise about specific accomplishments works wonders. Recall how you felt when someone praised you for a job well done? That's how others feel, too, when they receive such praise. How did you feel toward the person who praised you? Positively? Of course. And that's how other people feel, too. We all naturally gravitate toward people who think we have done something good and who tell us so.

5. Control Wisely How You Express Negative Feelings, Especially Anger

If you are giving off signals on a fairly continual basis

that you are out of control emotionally, building positive relationships with your coworkers will be difficult. People don't like to get too close to a vehicle—say an automobile—that is out of control. They feel the same way about people who appear to be out of control emotionally.

Anger is a powerful emotion that every person must learn to control in order to function in a healthy and productive manner and build positive relationships with other people. If you are given to "flying off the handle," most folks will not want to get any closer to you than the length of an eleven-foot pole.

I have a rather firm hunch that every single person gets angry from time to time. What shall we do about this? The question is not whether we will become angry. The question, rather, is how we will deal with our anger, at work and elsewhere.

Consider anger as a large ball you can hold in your hand. What are some things you could do with that ball of anger?

One thing you could do is to swallow it. The idea of swallowing a ball seems rather strange, but often we do just that with our anger and think it's the right thing to do. We swallow our anger, just as we might swallow a ball. The results are as ludicrous and as catastrophic to our physical, mental, and spiritual well-being as swallowing a large rubber ball would be. Depression of our minds and spirits plus physical difficulties themselves result when we simply swallow our anger, thinking we are hiding it from others. That's not a wise solution.

A second thing you could do with this ball is to take it and throw it as hard as you can at someone, perhaps the one who made you angry. Such aggressive physical or verbal displays of anger rarely if ever help anyone. Such displays are sometimes amusing in two-year-olds but always embarrassing in adults. Often we are ashamed of our behavior once we have come to our senses. Generally people create another whole set of problems for themselves and others when they throw this ball of anger at someone else.

Inappropriate expressions of anger get folks in trouble at work, just as at other places. Explosions of anger can create a mushroom cloud that lingers in the workplace for a long time.

A third thing you could do with that ball of anger is to find a friend and play catch with him or her. When you are angry at work, I hope you can find someone who will hear you out as you talk about your angry feelings. Such a game of catch with anger is a quite constructive way of dealing with it. Talking about anger generally is a way of dispelling it and helping us to move on to deal constructively with the problem itself.

A fourth thing you could do with this ball of anger is to score with it. I don't know what sort of ball you have been thinking of, but think of this ball as a basketball. You can take this big ball of anger, shoot it at the basketball goal, and score with it. This image is a way of talking about channeling our anger into constructive activity.

What constructive things can you do with your anger? Can you work it out on that problem that has frustrated you? Can you let your anger energize you into positive action? Can you let your anger motivate you to correct a frustrating situation? If you are angry at a person you can identify, can you blow up privately and then use some of the leftover energy to go to that person and talk out the problem? If the person has criticized you, the criticism might be his own misdirected expression of anger. He may have taken out on you his anger at someone else.

Another thing you could do with this ball of anger would be to take it to the edge of the sea, place the ball in the hands of God, and let Him cast it as far away as the east is from the west, so that it sinks into the depths, never to be seen or heard from again. Forgiveness is the word for this experience of cleansing.

A psychiatrist in the Bible study class I teach told of a sign he saw in a mental hospital. The sign asked, "Do you want revenge, or do you want to get well?" A good question, isn't it? Ask yourself that question about any crossed-up relationships you have with people at work. A lot of folks fail to develop healthy relationships because they keep insisting on getting revenge. Getting revenge can take the form of a cold war as well as a real blow-up.

Forgiveness is an important, truly healthy way of dealing with our anger. It's as important in the close confines of the workplace as it is at other places in your life.

6. Give Other People the Space They Need

Be careful when you're seeking to reach out to others and build positive relationships with them. Leave them enough space in which to breathe.

Some people have been burned by those who have called them their "friends." Thus, they may be wary about expressions of friendship, attempts to build relationships. People who've been burned by such encounters need space in which to live. Every person does, in fact. Be careful of appearing *too* interested in others' concerns. Such interest can turn to gossip or meddling, or it may be interpreted as such.

A sea gull perching on an ocean-front wall will leave plenty of space—a foot or so—between him and the next sea gulls. Even sea gulls need living space, and human beings need space even more.

7. Listen

The greatest demonstration of respect we can offer to acknowledge how much we value any person is to listen to what the person has to say. It's often been noted that God must have had something specific in mind when He made us with one mouth and two ears. Perhaps having two ears versus one mouth is an indication of our need to listen twice as much as we talk. Or perhaps it indicates that since listening is twice as difficult as talking, we need two ears rather than one.

An expert on communication has pointed out, "It really is not difficult to learn to listen, just unusual."[9] Whether listening is unusual or difficult, it opens the door to building positive relationships with others. When we listen, we show we truly care. After all, we could be using that time to dump *our* burdens and cares on that person. Instead, listening is giving to another the precious gift of time—our time.

A word of caution. Be careful not to spend work time "building relationships" to the neglect of doing the *work* expected of you. Breaks and lunch provide the extended periods of time that may be needed for conversations that lead to building positive relationships. Further, the basic idea behind the other methods mentioned has more to do with adjusting our attitudes than with calling for extensive conversations.

Relating to Your Supervisor

I am about to give you an important statement about building a positive relationship with your supervisor. The statement may appear crass and undignified, but the principle it contains is all-important in human relationships. This principle certainly applies to your relationship with your supervisor, but it also applies to your relationship with people in general. Here is the statement: *Give others what they need, and they in turn will be more likely to give you what you need.*[10]

Of course, you could view this principle as a straight business proposition—a cold, impersonal exchange of value for value. If that's the way you view it, that's okay with me, for it is still useful as an operating principle. But it's also possible—and helpful—to view this principle as a statement of warm human relationships rather than simply a description of a coldly impersonal exchange of services.

Your supervisor, you see, is a human being, with wants, needs, hopes, fears, worries, regrets, prejudices—just like everyone else, even you. He wants happiness in his work, too, just like you; and he may not be any happier in his job than you are in yours.

He's responsible to his supervisor, or to the stockholders. Or, if he's in business for himself, he's taken on himself the risks of ownership. He is probably trying to figure out from week to week if not day to day how he can help the business to survive and prosper. The survival and prosperity of his business is not a sure thing, and he knows it.

Your supervisor has certain goals to accomplish. How will he get them done? The reason you've been employed comes in right here. You've been employed to help your supervisor achieve a certain portion of the goals he or she is trying to accomplish. You'll help yourself in your relationship with your supervisor if you will learn that important truth.

Now, look back at that important statement of human relationships: *Give others what they need, and they in turn will be more likely to give you what you need.* Have you ever given much thought to what your supervisor needs? Have you ever gone a step farther to see how your effective performance of your job gives him or her what he or she needs? What are your supervisor's goals? To what extent are you working to help him achieve them?

Please note that the issue at stake here is not your bowing and scraping to your supervisor, engaging in a bootlicking routine. That's detestable—sometimes necessary, I grant you, but detestable just the same! What is at stake here is how you might perform your job in the manner that best fits in with the tasks the organization has assigned to your supervisor.

It's a simple fact of life: *We appreciate people who help us achieve our goals.* Do you want to build a positive relationship with your supervisor? Then seek to do your job in a way that helps him accomplish his goals. That's the first suggestion you need to act on to build a positive relationship with him or her.

What else can you do to build a positive relationship with the person who supervises you? Another important answer to this question is that you need to be open and honest in your relationships with that person.

A key ingredient in all positive human relationships is *trust.* If your supervisor perceives you to be a person who can be trusted, you will be able to get his support for almost any reasonable request. You will be able to explain to his satisfaction almost any mistake you may make.

On the other hand, suppose your supervisor perceives you to be a person who cannot be trusted. Suppose he considers you to be always looking for ways to cut corners. Suppose he thinks you will shave the truth to your advantage. If these statements describe your supervisor's perception of you—and especially if you can't explain the actions on which he has based his negative judgment—you have an uphill battle that you will inevitably lose.

If you are seen as a person of integrity, be thankful. What if you're not seen that way, though? Then you need to begin now to act with complete integrity. If you feel you have a black or even grey mark on your supervisor's opinion of you, you may need to take the initiative and clear up any misunderstandings about your past behavior.

Is trying to make a fresh start worth the risk? Yes, for if the word on you is bad, your opportunities are limited. The worst-case scenario, in fact, is that your days are numbered. And, yes, trying to make a fresh start is worth the risk because you have so much to gain. A good name is important. The lack of a good name indeed does make us "poor indeed," as Shakespeare wrote.[11]

So, to build a positive relationship with your supervisor, take these actions:

1. Try to help your supervisor achieve his or her goals.

2. Be a trustworthy person, a person of real integrity.

And, consider this suggestion, outlandish as it may seem:

3. If you ever catch your supervisor doing something right, tell him so. Chances are your boss needs praise for his work as much as you need praise for yours.[12] And, if your relationship currently is built on your finding fault with almost everything he does, you don't have much of a chance of building a positive relationship. Positive relationships are built on positive feedback—catching the other person doing something right—rather than on negative feedback—always looking for what the other person is doing wrong.

How can you keep such positive feedback about your supervisor's work from being perceived as simply "buttering him up"? Follow these three guidelines for offering compliments:

• *Be sincere* in your praise. If it's not so, don't say it. Remember, you're trying to be open and honest.

• *Be specific* about what you are offering praise for. Be able to point to one specific, definable action as the basis for the praise you offer. The first time or two you offer general praise, it may be accepted. Before long, although you may be sincere in your praise, your supervisor will begin to feel that you are trying to do a snow job on him. Being specific attaches meaning to praise.

• *Be honest with yourself.* Be sure that you are offering the compliment as one human being to another rather than as a weapon for manipulating your boss to think more of you. Be clear in your motives. Admittedly, the line here is rather fine. But you need to work diligently on this one or your attempt at praise may well fall flat. It's going to be tough enough to offer a compliment to your supervisor. Don't make it harder by trying to manipulate him. Positive relationships are built on honesty, not manipulation.

Personalizing This Idea

An item in the newspaper caught my eye some time ago. The brief article was about a beauty contest. At the question-and-answer time, one of the contestants was asked this question: "If you were shipwrecked and alone on a desert island, what would you miss most about your present day life?" The young woman brought down the house when she replied, "If I was alone on a desert island, I'd miss people more than anything else."

I'm not putting you on; she really said it! I'm looking at the newspaper clipping right now, in fact.[13]

Her answer, for all its wide-eyed innocence, is profoundly meaningful. At the same time that our relationships with people bring us so many problems, people also bring us so much joy. As Dennis Wholey, author and former television show host, says, "It is the people in our lives who bring us the most happiness."[14]

At your place of work, you may be miserable because of negative relationships with your coworkers or with your supervisor. Perhaps you identify quite well with this famous line from the *Peanuts* cartoon: "I love humanity; it's people I can't stand." Your place of work may seem almost to be hell on earth because of the people with whom and for whom you work. You're not likely to be very happy in your job if your relationships with the people there are sour.

So, because people are so important in making us happy or unhappy—at work as well as almost everywhere else—you need to consider carefully this chapter's suggestions. Review the major points. See if putting them into practice might help make your job more pleasant and satisfying.

Key Points

1. Relate to fellow employees.
   Review the seven suggested ways of relating.
2. Relate to your supervisor.
   Review the three suggested ways of relating.

Notes

1. Nashville *Banner*, July 18, 1987.

2. Michael Maccoby, *Why Work: Leading the New Generation* (New York: Simon and Schuster, 1988), 62.

3. Auren Uris, *Thank God It's Monday* (New York: Thomas Y. Crowell Company, 1974), 149.

4. James E. Dittes, *When Work Goes Sour* (Philadelphia: The Westminster Press, 1987), 83.

5. John Sutherland Bonnell, *No Escape from Life* (New York: Harper and Row, 1958), 193, citing Ian Maclaren.

6. Paul Hersey and Kenneth Blanchard, *Management of Organizational Behavior*, second edition (Englewood Cliffs, N. J.: Prentice-Hall, Inc., 1972), 77-78, citing Rensis Likert, *New Patterns of Management* (New York: McGraw-Hill Book Company, 1961), 7.

7. Bruce Larson, *No Longer Strangers* (Waco, Tex.: Word Books, Publisher, 1971), 89-90.

8. Bart McDowell, "Hungary: Enchanting Homeland of a Tough, Romantic People," *National Geographic*, 139 (April 1971): 479.

9. Stuart Chase in collaboration with Marian Tyler Chase, *Power of Words* (New York: Harcourt, Brace and Company, 1954), 165.

10. Adapted from Robert Conklin, *How to Get People to Do Things* (Chicago: Contemporary Books, Inc., 1979), 7.

11. *Othello*, Act III, Scene 3, lines 155-161.

12. See Kenneth Blanchard and Norman Vincent Peale, *The Power of Ethical Management* (New York: William Morrow and Company, Inc., 1988), 103.

13. *The Shreveport Times* (May 26, 1965).

14. Dennis Wholey, *Discovering Happiness: Personal Conversations About Getting the Most Out of Life* (New York: Avon Books, 1986), 6.

5
Handle Criticism Carefully

A television commercial pictures an older man, obviously the supervisor, in a rather heated conversation with a younger employee. In unmistakable language, the supervisor tells the worker that the worker has made a costly mistake. The employee should have used a certain method of sending some important information to a branch office. Instead, he stupidly had used another method which was much slower. The employee's mistake would prevent the company from completing an important transaction in time to meet a deadline. The employee should have known better.

An interesting aspect of this interchange is that while the supervisor blamed the employee, the supervisor was the one really at fault. The supervisor had failed to give clear and adequate instructions. No matter, though. As happens all too frequently, the criticism came to the employee, who "should have known."

Has anything like that ever happened to you on *your* job? Unless you've never worked a day in your life, are absolutely perfect, or have had supervisors who were either perfect at relating to employees or completely uncaring about how a job got done, it's happened.

Criticism is a fact of life for almost every person who works—or just lives. Everyone who works has to deal with criticism. It's an unwritten part of every job description. Supervisors give criticism. "Performance review" is a sophisticated word for criticism, as you likely have figured out by now.

Fellow employees also criticize. A fellow worker may say, "I don't mean to be critical, but . . . ." When you hear those words, you can be rather sure that someone is about to unload some criticism, whether light or heavy. These words often signal that a velvet-covered brick or just a brick is about to be launched in someone's direction. That someone may deserve it, and it may ultimately turn out to be quite helpful. It's still criticism, however.

People who work directly with customers get plenty of criticism, justified or unjustified. Pity the poor sales clerk, for example, who receives criticism that often really should go to the establishment's management.

It happens everywhere. The most accessible person generally is the one who receives the criticism. That may be you. Almost everybody, it seems, has a better idea about how you can do your work or go about your life than you do.

I once lived on a road that was under destruction—that's right, destruction, though the signs said "Under Construction." As my car struggled through the mud early one morning, the wheels finally became mired down in it, unable to go forward or backward.

Some road construction workers were at work nearby. They saw the problem and came to help.

I'm sorry to say that in my frustration I unloaded some choice criticism on a worker who had been running a piece of heavy equipment. The guy had come to help me, but in my anger at the situation I unloaded on him. Criticizing him helped me feel better, but not for long.

You see, I was talking to a fellow who had a healthy perspective on himself and his job. He probably didn't have a high school education, but he knew well how to handle criticism. As the worker graciously helped me free my car, he informed me in a kind manner what I knew but had pushed to the far corner of my mind. He just ran the bulldozer. He hadn't decided how a particular task was going to be accomplished or how many weeks or months it was going to take. He was just there doing his job. And furthermore, he hadn't made it rain!

I had to admit he was absolutely right about the whole situation. Someone else should have received my criticisms. And I should have kept some of them to myself, for a good part of the situation could be explained by these words: "That's just the way life is." Roads need to be repaired, and life is so structured that it rains in south Louisiana--often and a lot at the time. Criticizing doesn't help; that's just the way at least a part of life is.

Lots of folks often appear to take other people as their "improvement projects." I've met a person or two who claimed to be gifted at being critics. They claimed they could spot what was wrong every time, but they didn't claim to know how to correct it. Believe it or not, they boasted about that alleged "gift" of criticism. Some gift. Most folks aren't that forthright about it. Such would-be critics are all around us. Deliver me—and you—from such people, and may their tribe decrease! In fact, if all the people who thought they were supposed to be critics of the rest of us were laid end to end, the rest of us would be a whole lot more comfortable.

Our critics aren't about to go away voluntarily. And some of them—like supervisors, fellow employees, and customers—simply come with the job. Therefore, what you are going to have to do on any job, if you're going to be happier in it, is learn how to handle criticism carefully.

How do you deal with criticism? How *should* you deal with it? Here are some handles for handling criticism with care.

Expect Criticism

I've already more than hinted at this first suggestion. Sometimes people are surprised when they find others standing in judgment over them and perhaps even offering criticism that is harsh and/or undeserved.

We should not be surprised, however, when criticism comes. The tendency to criticize is so prevalent among human beings that Jesus in the Bible even had to admonish would-be critics, "Judge not."[1]

Even the most revered folks get criticized. Perhaps I should say that *especially* the most revered folks get criticized. Here's a question for you. Which President of the United States was called a hypocrite and was jeered by crowds as he traveled down the street? Did you answer, "all of them"? You're probably correct. You might be surprised to learn that George Washington, the father of our country, received this treatment himself.[2]

People will criticize us from good motives and bad. They will criticize us when we deserve it and when we don't. They may sugarcoat their criticism with faint or lavish praise, or they may simply hit us with the brass knuckles of harsh criticism. The result is the same.

People criticize. Why? It's simple. Supervisors, fellow employees, and customers are all human. Human beings criticize. Criticism is the critic's way of trying to remake the world to fit an image of what the critic thinks it ought to be. People like to do that. Although they may not like to criticize, they think someone who has authority over them expects them to engage in criticism. Whatever the case, we should not be surprised when we are a part of the world that some critic wants or needs to remake.

And why should we think we are exempt? Have we reached perfection on our jobs or in our lives? Likely not. We may strive toward perfection. We may work hard. However, how hard we try and how hard we work are not in question here. The fact is, since no one is perfect, you and I should expect criticism.

Don't Take Criticism Personally

Even when criticism is directed at you personally and even if the criticism is a vicious personal attack, there's one action you should never take. *Don't* take criticism personally. Refuse to allow anyone, no matter what his or her level of authority, that kind of control over your life. You are a person of genuine worth. As the saying goes, "God don't make no junk." *Whatever your shortcomings may be at a certain point of time about certain job skills, you are now, have always been, and will always be a person of genuine worth.* Nothing you do can change that. Nothing anyone can say can change that. No one has the right to try to destroy that all-important idea. In fact, no one has the power to do so, really—unless *you* allow it to happen.

So, shield your *self* from the daggers of personal criticism. Don't let those sharp, destructive words inside your head. You may have to hear the words. You may need to learn from them. You may need to assess your behavior to try to figure out why such criticism is being directed your way. Based on those critical words directed at you personally, you may need to make changes in the way you do things.

But you don't have to let words of personal criticism into the heart of your life. You *must* not let them distort or destroy who you are. You, along with every other human being, *make* mistakes, but *you* are not a mistake. You must not permit criticism, even personal criticism, to cloud that fundamental truth about you.

Now, the kind of criticism I mean by personal criticism is the kind that suggests you are worthless and no-good to the core. Hopefully you will have to hear very little of that sort of criticism from anyone. If you do, don't believe it. You're better than that.

Sometimes people have programmed themselves to take any and all suggestions for improvement—in job skills, say—as a personal attack on their innermost selves. You'll help yourself a great deal if you will refuse to view specific guidance and instruction about your job skills as being criticisms of you personally. How can you do this? You can do this by learning to distinguish between criticisms of *who you are*—which are unacceptable—and criticisms of *what you are doing*. Why is the difference important? Criticisms of what you are doing focus on areas that can be identified objectively and possibly changed. Criticisms of who you are deal with matters that are more subjective and not as readily available to change. Criticisms of who you are deal with your identity itself, with the core of your personality.

For example, just because you right now are unable to use your computer as well as your supervisor would like you to use it does not mean you are not a fine person. Some fine people can't use a computer. And, some people who can use a computer are the kind of folks you wouldn't want to invite into your home, or even your car. You'd cringe, in fact, at having to share the same bus seat with them. Being able to use a computer (or a typewriter or a bulldozer) and being a fine person have no relationship.

I've spent a good bit of my life in school. When I returned to graduate school after several years in the world of work, I had to confront again the reality of tests.

What follows tests? Grades. What are grades? Grades are another word for criticism.

In earlier days, I tended to consider a grade on *my work* as a grade on *me*. Thanks, though, to some maturity I had gained as an adult, when I returned to graduate school I determined that I would allow grades to constitute evaluations only of *what I had learned*. I decided not to allow grades to be evaluations of *who I was*.

Thus, I chose to consider myself to be always an "A" person, even though my grade report might show a different letter grade. By the same token, you need to see yourself as a top-notch *person* even though your supervisor's evaluation of your *job skills* may be different.

So, don't take criticism personally. In fact, you and I should simply disregard some criticism and keep on plugging away. Some critics are simply mean, misguided, ignorant, or all three. I know those are tough words, but I believe they're true. We can deal best with some criticism by keeping it at arm's length.

Abraham Lincoln mastered this technique. This great man knew what receiving criticism was like. He received plenty of it. The word "vicious" fits well some of the criticism Lincoln received. The critics were aiming at Lincoln personally.

Lincoln likely would never have accomplished what he did and risen to such greatness had he not learned to deal with criticism and not take it personally. These powerful words describe how he handled the barbs of criticism fired his way:

> If I were to try to read, much less to answer, all the attacks made on me, this shop might as well be closed for any other business. I do the very best I know how—the very best I can; and I mean to keep on doing so until the end. If the end brings me out all right, then what is said against me won't matter. If the end brings me out wrong, then ten angels swearing I was right would make no difference.[3]

Keep Your Eyes on the Criticism— Not the Critic, Not Yourself

When someone criticizes you ("when," not "if"), force yourself to give your attention to the criticism itself. You've just decided, you recall, not to take the criticism personally.

And, although most of us would like to deflect any criticism and blame the critic for saying anything at all to us, that approach is unproductive. Here's why.

Let's say the criticism is deserved and given in the right spirit and for a good motive, say, to help us improve our job skills so we will be more productive. Where's the gain for us if we become angry at the person who has criticized us? Refusing to accept the criticism cuts ourselves off from the increased happiness that would come from doing a better job.

What if the criticism is given in the wrong spirit and for a bad motive? Again, we'll help ourselves if we will force ourselves to focus on the criticism, not the critic, be he or she supervisor, fellow employee, or customer.

The problem with the critic who criticizes in the wrong spirit, for a bad motive, and with poor technique is simply that he or she is a lousy critic. We can still learn from the criticism even if the critic has delivered it with all the finesse of the proverbial bull loose in a china shop or a butcher masquerading as a surgeon. The situation may be rather messy and with a lot of broken pieces to pick up. Nevertheless, we can still gain some benefit from the criticism.

Being a sharp-eyed reader, you probably noticed that I left out the word "undeserved" in the discussion in the previous two paragraphs. You likely will get some undeserved criticism. What do you do then? Let's digress a moment to deal with that problem. Here are some possibilities, each of which will work in different circumstances.

(1) You could dismiss the undeserved criticism from your mind, considering the source. Brooding on a wrong done to you will hurt only you. Forgiveness is healthy. Forgiving someone who has wronged you shows strength, not weakness; toughness, not softness. Holding a grudge will destroy you, not the critic. Trying to "get back at" the critic generally will only perpetuate the cycle of wrong. People tend to hit back even if they hit first to begin with. (2) You could con-

front the critic and ask for the evidence. If your critic is a human being of at least average reasoning power and at least average sensitivity to people, this approach has a good chance of bearing fruit. However, if your critic is a manipulator who would feel threatened by an adult-to-adult discussion, taking this course may be risky. Assuming your critic is the former, one mark of a good critic is the ability to be specific and factual about criticism. If your critic can't be specific and factual, you will know. And, the critic himself may come to see the injustice in his remarks. At the very least, such a confrontation may leave the critic with some uneasiness about his judgment.

What if the critic is a manipulator, particularly if he or she is a manipulator with power over your job? Then you obviously need to proceed carefully. At every encounter, you would be wise to try to move the criticism to specifics and away from generalities. That won't solve the problem, I admit, but even some manipulators recognize the power of facts. If this person is a coworker, there may come the time when you need to get your supervisor to give you an evaluation of your work at the points where the manipulator is attacking. If your supervisor thinks you are doing a good job, you can begin to discount much of the ravings of the manipulative critic. As a last resort, you may need to ask for help to work out the relationship roadblock that exists between you and the manipulative critic.

Learn from the Criticism

Some unknown wit has suggested we ought to learn from every bad experience, else why go through it to begin with. That certainly applies to criticism.

When you find yourself on the receiving end of criticism, it's time to listen to find out whether the critical words contain something important that requires action. We've already established that all criticism is not important. Some criticism should be disregarded. It doesn't apply. It tells more about the critic than about you.

But what about the criticism that *does* contain truth, that *is* important, and that *does* apply to you? The criticism may have been delivered clumsily. Perhaps your supervisor shouted at you and hurt your feelings. Perhaps he humiliated you before a fellow employee in delivering the criticism. Both of those situations are unfortunate. There's no denying that such things hurt. But maybe, too, there's a grain of truth in even clumsily-delivered criticism that needs your attention and action.

Remember, one of the important points of this book's message about finding happiness in a job you sometimes can't stand is that *you* are responsible for *your* actions. You're not responsible for the actions of others, but you *are* responsible for *your* actions and your *reactions* to the actions of others. We can't use others as an excuse for not following through on the actions we need to take.

Not too long ago, I was on the receiving end of criticism. I didn't like what I heard. It didn't seem like me. It didn't fit the way I perceived myself acting. And, the criticism did not cite specific instances or really give me enough data to make a lot of changes.

How did I react to all of this criticism? I won't deny it; I became angry. Furthermore, I had good cause for my anger, in my opinion (naturally).

After I was able to deal constructively with my anger about the unfortunate event, however, I could think a bit more rationally about the criticism. I still did not agree with the criticism totally, but I began to ask myself what particular aspects of my behavior might have led the person who criticized me to evaluate me in the manner in which he had. I identified an action or two. I then decided I needed to keep a close watch on some ways in which I was performing my job. So, I learned from the criticism even though the way in which it was delivered was not as helpful as it could have been and even though I still don't fully agree with the criticism.

Ask for Assistance

Say you have heard the criticism, discovered there's some truth in it, and decided it's something you *can* change and *want* to change. What next? If you already know what steps to take, go to it. But what if you don't know what to do?

If you would like to make improvements but want some help in knowing how to make them, the person to ask first for assistance might well be the person who helped you identify the problem to begin with. Perhaps that person sees how to start finding a solution even as he or she saw the problem. At least, asking for the critic's help will reveal something important about you: you are capable of handling criticism in a healthy and positive manner. Criticism doesn't destroy you or cause you to become your own defense attorney. You take criticism as an opportunity to learn and perhaps to improve. You are one of those special people who has learned to handle criticism with just the right amount of care.

Personalizing This Idea

I'm intrigued by some advice that Walter Anderson, editor of *Parade*, gave about handling criticism. He wrote that the person being criticized should say "thank you" to the critic.[4] When I suggested this approach to a few of my friends, they rather scoffed at the idea, to put it mildly. Of course, that shows the kind of friends I have. It also shows that our natural human response is to react negatively to criticism. We find accepting criticism very difficult. Most of us rank accepting criticism right down there with crawling around on the garbage dump. Criticism sticks in our minds, hearts, and souls.

As Walter Anderson says, "If today you heard a hundred words of praise and one word of criticism, which would be on your mind tonight?" His next words were, "Me too."[5]

And I say, "Me too." If you don't say, "Me too," thus agreeing about the depressing power of criticism, then I envy you; and you don't need to do a thing about this chapter. It's not for you. You already know how to handle criticism far better than most folks do.

If perchance you know what it means to be burdened down by the heavy weight of criticism, however, then this chapter *is* for you. I hope you'll find the suggestions helpful the next time you face criticism—whether deserved or undeserved, whether delivered by a sensitive surgeon or someone akin to a madman wielding an ax.

Before you leave this idea about handling criticism, recall a time when you yourself were a critic of someone else. You likely would not have considered yourself a critic or have called what you did criticism, but you fulfilled the definition. You evaluated some aspect of that person's life, decided you knew a better way, and proceeded to tell it to that person, hopefully in a gracious and kind manner, but maybe not.

Perhaps this person was very close to you and you cared deeply about him or her. You were not trying to run the person's life or manipulate him or her to "see things your way." You just wanted the best for that person, and you wanted to give some guidance toward achieving it.

How did you hope the person on the receiving end of the criticism would react? Didn't you hope that person would not take your criticism personally but would accept it graciously, learn from it, and apply it in a helpful manner? Likely that's exactly what you hoped. Does that thought tell you something about how you should accept criticism from others?

The "Golden Rule of Accepting Criticism" can be stated

like this: *Accept criticism from others as you would have them accept criticism from you.*

And how's that?

• Expect it; after all, no one is perfectly on target *all* the time.

• Don't take criticism personally.

• Focus on the criticism itself—not the critic and not yourself.

• Learn what you can from the criticism, and apply what you learn.

• Even ask your critic for help if you need it.

• If you can bring yourself to do it, say "thank you."

That's how.

Key Points

1. Expect criticism.
2. Don't take criticism personally.
3. Keep your eyes on the criticism—not the critic, not yourself.
4. Learn from the criticism.
5. Ask for assistance.

Notes

1. Matthew 7:1.
2. Dale Carnegie, *How to Enjoy Your Life and Your Job* (New York: Pocket Books, 1985), 56.
3. Ibid., 62.
4. Walter Anderson, *Courage Is a Three-Letter Word* (New York: Fawcett Crest, 1986), 260.
5. Ibid., 14.

6
Master the Tension of Stress

Ann roused with a start. She had suddenly realized that the soft music she was hearing was not part of her dream. Her clock radio had gone off, and the clock insisted it was time to get up. For an instant, she tried to convince herself it was Saturday, but to no avail. She knew immediately the day was definitely Tuesday.

Ann dragged herself out of bed and trudged to the bathroom. In a few moments, she emerged to shuffle to the children's bedroom to awaken them. After the usual groans and protests, the two of them stumbled out of bed. They moved as sleepily as she did.

As the children began to get dressed, Ann headed to the kitchen to prepare breakfast. At least she could do *that* for her children before they all went in separate directions for the day. Ann glanced at the kitchen clock and knew the word for the day was "hurry."

In the midst of Ann's breakfast preparation, the sharp, loud noise of squabbling came from the direction of the children's bedroom. Ann hoped it would subside. When it didn't, she made a quick trip to get the problem solved. As she hurried back to the kitchen, she heard the microwave beeping insistently. Sometimes it seemed to Ann that all she did all day, wherever she happened to be, was react to the noisy demands of people and electronic gadgets.

Before she called the children to breakfast, she took just a moment to sip some coffee and munch on a sweet roll. Then, glancing at the clock again, she called the children. First the nine-year-old and then the four-year-old, both children arrived at last, dawdling along the way as usual. Then they all gulped down their food.

Soon all three of them departed from the apartment. The nine-year-old walked to the bus stop to wait for the school bus. Ann dropped off the four-year-old at a day care center on her way to work.

As Ann fought the stop-and-go traffic, she recalled how much she dreaded the day's work. Since no one had been hired to fill the vacancy in her section, Ann was having to do not only her work but also part of the work of the "dearly departed." What's more, today was the day her supervisor expected to see a completed major project he had assigned Ann only the day before. This project was out of Ann's area, and so she wasn't as familiar with the work as she would have been with a task in her own regular job assignment.

Ann had hoped to be farther along on the project than she was so she could breathe easier today. She probably would have to work through lunch. She would just *have* to, since her supervisor was such a stickler for details and deadlines. Ann would rather work through lunch than endure the ice-cold remarks of her supervisor.

Just then, Ann felt a bolt of resentment flash through her mind. *Too much to do, too little time, too high demands, too little understanding—that's what I have to deal with day in and day out. I don't need this. I just don't know how much longer I can take this pressure.* Ann felt her stomach tighten as she parked the car. As she headed to her desk, she said to herself, *What a day this is going to be. I'll be glad when it's over.*

Ever had a day like that? Probably, and likely a whole lot worse. One word for what Ann was experiencing is *stress*. The very word can cause the very feelings it describes. The word *stress* itself may make us tighten up, feeling the pressure of some previous unpleasant experience and the dread of some time of reckoning yet to come.

The Basics of Stress

The stress experts distinguish two varieties of stress.[1] They call one variety *eustress. Eu* is a Greek word prefix meaning "good." So, one variety of stress is "good stress." This sort of stress mobilizes us for action. Eustress may be generated by a challenge within our powers—an exciting job assignment in an area in which we really like to work and for which we know we will receive affirmation, for example.

The second sort of stress is what we generally mean when we talk about stress. The stress experts call this *dis*tress. *Dis* is a Latin prefix meaning "bad." So, "distress" is bad stress. "Distress" is the kind of stress that creates problems for us. I'm going to keep on using the word "stress" the way we generally use it—meaning "distress," *bad* stress.

Why do human beings experience the kind of stress that is distress? Of course, plenty of people who lived before modern times had stress. Our modern life-style, however, certainly lends itself quite well to the stress experience. In fact, too well, and that's the problem you and I face, likely on a daily basis.

The stress response is really a valuable response for human beings to have. Our life-style, not the stress response itself, is the problem. The stress response, you see, is the body's way of preparing itself to deal physically with whatever the human being perceives as a threat.

Imagine one of your ancestors rounding a bend in the trail and coming face to face with a bear with her cub. The bear, of course, would have been none too happy about your ancestor's disturbing this bit of quality time with her cub.

That event would have put something of a damper on

your ancestor's day, too. Likely the bear began to make noises and movements that indicated she was about to attack. At that point, your ancestor would have had only two basic choices—fight the bear physically or flee from the bear physically. Sitting down and talking about the situation wasn't an option. Filling in the proper forms was not an option. Calling the security guard was not an option.

When your ancestor's mind recognized the problem and began in a split second to consider whether to flee or fight, his or her body's stress response kicked in automatically. Your ancestor's stress response mobilized the heart, lungs, muscles, and digestive system for action.

The choice was made pretty quickly, too. No stewing for days about what ought to be done. No committee meetings to discuss various options. No going upline to propose a possible response and to wait for an approval. No, your beloved ancestor had only a few seconds to decide to take on the bear or absent himself or herself from the bear's territory as quickly as possible. In either case, your ancestor took physical action rather soon—immediately—to utilize the vital stress response and save his or her life.

Note, the stress response worked rather handily when your ancestor was confronted by a bear or a tiger. But, as the saying goes, the times are changing; indeed, times *have* changed. Unlike your ancestor, you don't round a bend in the trail. You round a corner in the office building or factory, or you step off the elevator to the twelfth floor. And, the stressor you encounter is not a bear but a demanding supervisor or a disgruntled coworker or an unhappy customer. Or perhaps it's the regulations or "the system."

However, when you round that corner and face your own personal bear, your stress response still mobilizes your body for action in much the same manner in which your ancestor's body mobilized his for action. Your heart, lungs, muscles, and digestive system get ready for action—physical action.

Our current style of life and our current societal views do not permit you to take the same kind of physical action your ancestor could take with regard to the bear. Society doesn't look with favor on your running physically from the supervisor or the coworker or the customer. And where would you run to escape "the system"? Still less does society permit you to attack physically the boss or the coworker or the customer.

So, we in our day are victims of this reaction pattern inherent in our bodies. It does not matter in the long run whether we call ourselves victims of our bodies or of our lifestyles. Whatever the answer, the stress response gets us all revved up physically, but society won't let us take the actions for which the stress response has prepared our bodies. When the stress response is in operation, our physical energy is mobilized and ready to fight or flee from the threat. We're unable, though, to use this physical preparation in the way nature intended.

What happens to all of this physical energy? We can't just pull the plug on it and drain it from ourselves, like draining water from a bathtub or letting air out of a tire. What happens to it, then? This energy stays inside of us, physically, and builds up in our tissues themselves. The tenseness we feel in our bodies when we are "under stress" is this unexpended physical energy. It's trapped inside of us, and we're trapped in there with it. Sometimes it can get very crowded in there, so packed that stress seems to be squeezing the very life out of us.

Stress—meaning distress—is one factor that makes people unhappy with their jobs. That's not news to us, of course. For whatever it's worth, however, studies have confirmed this word we already knew by experience.[2]

Before we look at what we can do to master the tension of stress at work, let's identify some of the aspects of our work that give rise to the stress response. Unless you work at a real, live zoo, you likely don't encounter real, live bears. The bears are waiting for you at work nevertheless.

Some Sources of Stress on the Job

What "bears" do you face at work?

Too Much Work to Do

Quantitative work overload is a fancy name for having too much work to do. Whether a person actually has too great a volume of work to do or just feels he or she does is beside the point. If one *feels* he has too much to do, he will experience the stress of work overload whatever the efficiency experts say about his job being manageable.

Quantitative work overload may be a source of the stress you feel. Productivity is such an important word in American business and industry. Sometimes the pressure is great to beat the accomplishments of last year, last month, or last week. It's only natural for management to seek to get the most for the personnel dollar by turning out the highest volume of work possible with the least people. So, corporations often try to increase productivity by assigning more work to fewer people.

A body—a person—can only do so much work. Even machines, in fact, can only do so much work. The computer system used in the business in which I work flashes a message on the screen sometimes that says something like this: PAUSE: SYSTEM OVERLOADED. The computer system then refuses to accept any more data. The machine seems to be saying, "I've had all of this that I can take. Don't give me any more work for a while. Let's take a break." When this message is displayed, try as we might we can't get the computer to accept any more data. And so we stop forcing the issue. What happens then? Our company has the choice of either accepting that this volume of work is the limit that can be done or making plans to get more computer equipment.

Unfortunately, determining how much work a human being can be expected to do is not that simple and clear cut. Or at least a human being's stress signals don't seem to get the same level of attention from an employer that a machine's overload signals generate.

Stress reactions, though, are the body's way of flashing the warning that the system is overloaded and that some relief is needed. Perceiving that you have too great a volume of work to do in too short a time can cause such an overload. Unlike the computer system, we may force ourselves—or be "motivated" by others—to do more. Sooner or later the wear and tear on the human being will show itself. This condition is a major source of the pressure people feel on the job, in fact.[3]

Work Too Complicated for Your Present Skill Level

Another sort of work overload is qualitative work overload. This kind of overload occurs when workers must perform tasks that exceed their knowledge and skills at that particular time. New jobs or unfamiliar elements of present jobs may generate in us the feeling that the work is too complicated. That feeling may range from vague uneasiness to immobilizing panic. Whether or not we acknowledge this feeling of qualitative work overload, it's still there, generating stress.

Do you remember when you began to learn to drive a car? So many instructions to remember, so many problems to watch for, so many levers to adjust and pedals to push and buttons to pull. Likely you felt a considerable amount of tenseness until you mastered the operation. When we are asked to work beyond our present abilities and knowledge, we feel the same sort of stress.

A combination of quantitative overload and qualitative

overload is a common source of stress in administrative, sales, and entrepreneurial positions.[4] In fact, I suspect that this combination occurs in almost any job at some point.

Uncertainty About Your Role at Work[5]

Remember how you approached your first day in your place of employment? You probably felt a high degree of uncertainty about at least the mechanical aspects of your job if not some concern about how you would fit in to this new work setting. When you began your job, you likely did not even know where the rest room was. You had to ask someone question after question about where to find a certain tool or how to do a certain task. Otherwise you ran the risk of embarrassing yourself or angering others because of some simple thing you "should have known." Every job has its own unique set of expectations and relationships.

You likely will experience stress at work if you are uncertain about the specific responsibilities of your job. Having a written job description helps, but no set of words on paper can go the distance toward helping you feel you know what you are *supposed* to do and what you *must not* do on your job. Experience—successful experience—is needed.

Even employees who have been on their jobs for a long while can face times of uncertainty about their specific job responsibilities. These times of uncertainty may occur when management changes, coworkers change, procedures are revised, or relationships with present management and coworkers are altered. How an employee adjusts to these changes tells the story about the strength of the stress response with which that employee must deal.

Feeling uncertain about one's work role can occur even when the work situation is stable. Some corporations and individual managers seem to have adopted a management style that aims at keeping employees off balance and under pressure.

An auto mechanic told me about the heavy stress load under which he lived and worked. In fact, the stress level affected his health. What was the source of the stress? He pinpointed the problem by saying to me, "You just don't know what pressure is until you have a boss standing over you, watching your every move." Such pressure builds resentment, adding to the stress.

One observer of the contemporary work scene has summarized the magnitude of the problem like this: "More people are being paid to watch other people than ever before."[6] It happens everywhere—the foreman in the factory, the security detail at the bank or department store, the "inspector" at various sorts of businesses. Such watching may be necessary, helpful in the long run, and justifiable, but it still lays a heavy burden of stress on many who are being watched.

Another cause of uncertainty about your work role may be inadequate feedback from those who matter, whether supervisor or coworkers, about how you are doing in accomplishing your job. We need to be able to judge for ourselves something of how well we are doing, of course, but almost everyone also needs the positive, helpful feedback that others give.

We experience stress when we're not sure what others think of our work, especially when we suspect they may not think we are doing very well. Every person wants respect and affirmation for a job well done. When we don't receive this respect and affirmation, we assume the worst, and the stress level rises.

Confinement in a Bureaucratic Straitjacket

Constant bombardment with rules and regulations can make the human spirit feel imprisoned. Policies and procedures can be curses or blessings. Most likely you've experienced them both ways. Policies and procedures, especially in the hands of a stickler for enforcing them, can be oppressive.

This straitjacket gets even tighter and more uncomfortable when policies and procedures conflict with themselves or with the way in which they are enforced. A company may have a procedure that calls for a job to be done a certain way in order to maintain safety standards. At the same time, the company's demand for productivity may call for ignoring or circumventing that safety standard. The employee may be challenged to ignore the safety standard to achieve greater production. That employee knows, however, that if an accident occurs, he or she will be beat over the head with the safety standard. The pressure is on, whatever the employee does.[7]

Conflict Between Work Roles and Other Roles[8]

An employee is not just a machine that shuts off at the end of the day or that has no other interests than performing assigned tasks. You have other roles and responsibilities. If your work and these other roles and responsibilities balance and mesh perfectly, then you can write this area off as a source of stress. But the rest of us may find this conflict between work roles and other roles to be a significant source of stress from time to time.

That's the case with Ann in the beginning of this chapter. She's a mother with two children. No husband is in the picture. She's the sole provider of care for those children. Concern for her children will be a part of her life at work every hour, most likely.

Ann probably feels a measure of guilt that she can't do more for her children and be with them more. She's already come to terms with the fact that she, at least, *can't* "have it all," at least not all at once.

Even if a husband were in the picture, Ann might have many of the same feelings. Or if the story were about Andy instead of Ann, he, too, might have some of the same feelings of conflict between his work role and his home role.

Differing values can be a source of conflict at work, too. Employers sometimes ask employees to do things that conflict with the ethical values employees hold. However prevalent such practices may actually be in the working world, employees feel that such things *do* happen. If an employee is working for a company and with coworkers who share basically the same values, there's no problem. But intense ethical conflict may occur when the values are significantly different. Stress results.

Decision-making

Another "bear" that employees face on the job is decision-making. The amount of stress that decision-making generates is determined by several factors, including these:

(1) How important are the consequences of the decision? The more people, money, and events are affected, the greater the stress.

(2) How complex is the decision? Obviously, the greater complexity of the decision, the greater the stress.

(3) How much information is available? Too much can be a problem, but too little is worse.

(4) Who is responsible for the decision? Generally speaking, the more people responsible for a decision, the less the stress on any one individual. And, as with surgery, a "major" decision is one for which I am responsible, and a "minor" one is one for which someone else is responsible!

(5) How much time is available? Generally, the less time to decide, the greater the stress.

(6) How strongly do you expect to make a good decision? The higher your expectation you will make a good decision, the lower the stress.[9] The self-fulfilling prophecy applies to the stress of decision-making.

(7) What sort of relationship do you feel you have with the

people to whom you are accountable? Decision-making is easier and less stress-inducing if you feel a significant amount of trust and affirmation from these people.

You probably can think of other sources of stress at work. One big determinant of the amount of stress you feel or don't feel is the manner in which your supervisor relates to you. Another source of stress is the general atmosphere in your workplace.

Beyond Diagnosis

More important than diagnosing the sources of the problem is finding some ways of remedying the situation. In fact, finding and practicing ways of mastering stress is *a lot* more important than identifying sources of stress, be they people, processes, or other such matters we must face at work.

A pioneer confronted by a bear was considerably more interested in finding how to master the situation than investigating the bear's ancestry. So, how can we master our own bear, the tensions of stress?

Eleven Ways to Master Stress

What can we do about stress? A lot of this book's ideas about being happier in the job you sometimes can't stand also apply to mastering stress. In addition to them, here are eleven more ways you can deal more effectively with the stress in your life. At least one of these ways, if not all of them, will help you. Why don't you zero in on at least two or three to which you will give some attention?

1. Recognize Stress When It Occurs

The first symptoms of stress generally go undetected. We may blame the malfunctioning of a bodily function—like the digestive system, for example—on something else. Most of us are reluctant to admit that stress is causing whatever physical difficulty we may be experiencing. Rather, we prefer to think that something mechanical has simply broken down in our bodies than think—or have others think—that we "couldn't take the pressure."

Or, we are irritated by little things. We find other people hard to get along with, for example, until we realize we're the ones who are causing the problem.

Or perhaps we constantly feel we are fighting a deadline. We may feel overwhelmed by our work—either the amount or the difficulty or both. Or maybe we're restless during the day and feel bored a good bit of the time. On the other hand, perhaps we find it hard to settle down and get to sleep at night; we're just too tense.

The first step toward mastering the tension of stress is to recognize stress when it occurs and admit it is affecting us. You may say, I know; I do that.

Do you? Consider a time when you experienced an all-too-rare break in your work on some occasion, perhaps at the completion of a major project. Perhaps you have had several days, maybe a week or so, of genuine relaxation while on vacation. (Okay, just suppose you had that kind of time, then.) Sometime during those days you may well have had the experience many have reported. You felt differently. That is, you felt good; you felt relaxed. You realized something was missing. What was missing was the feeling of stress you were not willing to admit you had been experiencing prior to that time. During the time of stress you had felt "normal," but the truth of the matter is that you had forgotten what "normal" actually is.[10]

So, what are some clues to stress? The amount of stress each person can deal with varies from person to person. Here are some signs of stress to watch for in yourself.[11] They don't necessarily signify stress all the time, but they are good clues. Check yourself out in these areas:

●Mood and disposition—feeling "hyper," overly excited; worrying; feeling insecure; having difficulty in sleeping;

feeling confused; being overly forgetful; feeling uncomfortable, ill-at-ease, or nervous.

•Bodily organs and functions—upset stomach, pounding heart, sweating for no apparent reason, moist hands, feeling light-headed or faint, having cold chills, "hot" face, dry mouth, ringing in ears, sinking feeling in the stomach.

•Muscles—shaking fingers and hands, inability to sit or stand still, twitches, headache, tense or stiff muscle, stuttering or stammering in speech, stiff neck.

Do any of these signs sound like old but unwelcome friends with which you are all-too-familiar? Then stress *may* be the cause. At least that's a possibility at which you ought to take a close look. You probably will want to ask your physician to help you evaluate the situation.

You won't get much farther in dealing with stress unless you learn to recognize it in yourself. Caution: don't always be taking your "Stress Quotient," trying to determine your stress temperature every hour on the hour. Remember, the only reason you want to recognize stress is so you can deal with it, not so you can graph how much more or less stress you feel today than you felt yesterday or one year ago today. Recognize when you have stress, but don't worry about trying to measure your stress level any more closely than that.

2. Curb Your Imagination

Our imaginations—what we *think* might happen—may be our biggest stressors. We can conjure up in our minds things that are much worse than will likely ever happen to us.

What we're talking about here, folks, is worry. It's a common human pastime. Worry, someone has said, is putting today's sun under tomorrow's cloud. One person told me she worried about her husband a lot, because he *never* got sick! I suppose she thought that all of the sicknesses of mankind must sooner or later descend upon him. She stood around waiting, wringing her hands, making herself miserable, fearful of that inevitable day. While she was doing that, though, her husband was having a blast, enjoying his good health.

But we keep worrying, unproductive as it is, illogical as it is. As one worrier put it, "Worry must do *some* good, because ninety-five percent of the things I worry about never happen."

You may have a very active imagination. Perhaps you have convinced yourself you just can't keep from thinking about "what might happen." Well, if you can't curb your imagination, at least try imagining good results instead of bad.

3. Distinguish Between Realistic and Unrealistic Expectations

Sometimes people hold themselves to some quite unrealistic expectations. Perhaps these expectations are in the *quantity* of the work you—or others—think you can do. Where did you or others get the idea you were supposed to be Superman or Wonder Woman?

Perhaps these unrealistic expectations are in the *quality* of the work. Where did you ever get the idea that you could be perfect? Where did others get the idea that since they are perfect, you ought to be perfect, too? It's unrealistic to expect to do a month's work in a week, perfectly.

Okay, perhaps you can, in a crunch, do an extraordinary amount of high quality work. You've done it, others have done it, I've done it. The need was there, and we just had to do it. But, please, give yourself a medal and a party and back off. You may be able to be Superman or Wonder Woman for a day or two, but not every day or even one day every week. Neither you nor anybody else should expect this of you.

We can burn the midnight oil for a while, but not forever. We and the oil will soon burn out.

Therefore, do the realistic. Don't hold yourself to meeting unrealistic expectations, at least not very often and not for very long. Negotiate the unrealistic with yourself or with others, if at all possible.

4. Manage Your Time Rather Than Letting Time Manage You

One wise but anonymous person has noted that the three greatest killers of Americans are not cancer, heart attacks, and accidents, but calendars, clocks, and telephones. These are the devices that often serve to imprison us and our time, however necessary and helpful these modern conveniences may be.

Of course, the choice is really not between managing our time or being managed by our time. Time doesn't manage anybody or anything. Time is simply a commodity of life. It's available to us to use as we will.

In the same way that you can't spend a dollar twice, you can't spend a minute of time twice. What's important is getting the most out of that minute of time by applying it to what is truly important at that moment. The best question you can ever ask yourself regarding time is this: *"What is the best use of my time right now?"*[12]

Chapter 7, "Get Organized," will give some guidance about organizing your time. You will learn there about listing your work priorities and following your list; and about giving prime time to prime tasks.

For now, simply recognize that you can manage some of the stress you may feel by giving attention to how you are going about your work. If you feel overloaded at work, you may well be able to help the situation by reorganizing how you are approaching your time.

5. Adjust Your Life-style

If certain actions and life patterns are laying a burden of stress on you, maybe you can do something about them. You don't have to be locked in to your present pattern of life. You need to fulfill your legitimate obligations, but you don't need to be boxed in by others' expectations.

Does mowing the lawn bug you? You might sell your house and live in an apartment or a condominium. I did. Does fighting traffic in your car annoy you? Start riding the bus to work rather than fighting traffic. It works for me.

Or, maybe you could get up earlier or later. Maybe you should stop watching television during meals if what's on the television raises your stress level and disturbs your digestion. Maybe you should choose a new lunch place from time to time, breaking the routine (sometimes abbreviated "rut") you are in.

On April 6, 1988, my family received the 1987 Christmas card from a friend. No, the late delivery was not the fault of the United States Postal Service. Our friend had mailed the card only a few days before.

We were so glad to hear from the friend that we joked only briefly about the sender's lateness. The next day, though, on April 7, 1988, we received another Christmas card. The card was from the same family! The sender explained that this one was the 1986 card that she had prepared to mail but had just never got around to it!

She's a very competent person, and he is a general in the Air Force (means he's very competent, too, in my book). I think she made some good adjustments in dealing with her time and obligations. Sure, we would have been delighted to have heard from the family more often. But what's the big deal about getting Christmas cards out on time? Letters enclosed with the family's 1986 and 1987 cards certainly testified to the busy and important lives they all—including the teenagers—had been living. As a matter of fact, we feel honored to be on their Christmas card list on any kind of regular basis, given all of the activities in which the family is involved. We will be glad to receive all future Christmas cards—whenever they may send them!

6. Get Some Physical Exercise of the Right Kind

Since the stress response was intended to result in physical movement, physical exercise is a way of using up stress energy. You will get the most stress relief if you exercise within a few hours of a stress-causing situation of which you are aware. But, since the body stores up the stress energy for about twenty-four hours, exercise within that longer period of time will still help.[13]

The *kind* of exercise to take is important. It could be physical labor. It could be sports.

A word of warning: Some kinds of exercise create additional stress rather than releasing it. Competitive sports may create additional stress, for example. Even individual sports like golf may create additional stress if one is too concerned about his score. Exercise you are undertaking for the purpose of reducing stress should be the kind that doesn't involve your ego.[14]

Here are some other ideas for releasing stress physically : (1) Squeeze or pound a tennis ball. (2) Punch a beanbag or throw darts, perhaps imagining the recipient of the blows or darts to be the person who has irritated you. (3) Scream (in private, of course; screaming tends to create too much stress for others when done in public). (4) Run in place. (5) Climb the stairs hurriedly, two at a time. (6) Take a quick walk around the building.[15] In fact, maybe walking should be a regular activity. It's great exercise and will help with more than stress.

Techniques have been developed to help people relax physically by relaxing their muscles. Something so simple as learning a breathing technique may help you to achieve relaxation and reduce stress. These techniques need not be considered weird or offbeat. They're really more in the area of helping people use to their greatest advantage the physical bodies God gave them. You may want to find out about these techniques and consider their appropriateness for you.[16]

7. Watch What You Eat and Drink

What you eat can contribute to the stress you feel.[17] Too much caffeine, too much refined sugar, too much salt, and too much cholesterol may be causing or aggravating the stress you feel. Need I say that smoking cigarettes and drinking alcoholic beverages can contribute to stress, too?

Consider caffeine, for example. Caffeine comes in coffee, cola, and chocolate. You need to be careful about how much of such things you eat or drink. How much is too much? The answer to that question varies, but the reasonable word on this is that consuming more than a couple of cups of coffee in a two-hour period is definitely raising your stress level. Also most Americans need to reduce their salt consumption significantly, since they use about three times more than the body requires per day.[18] Refined sugar—well, suffice it to say that most Americans have had too much of that already, and the size and shape they're in shows it.

On the other hand, some foods help to combat stress. Foods like fresh fruit and vegetables as well as whole grains provide nutrients needed to prevent stress and deal with it when it occurs.

8. Relax

Do you really need to stay tense, ready to go all the time? Give yourself permission to relax, and find ways to do so. What are some things you really like to do? Perhaps a hobby or some kind of special interest? Then make some time for it. Even dare to spend some time doing nothing. When you can do such things without feeling guilty, then you are on your way toward mastering the tension of stress.

9. See Your Doctor

It's possible you need some medical assistance in dealing with the physical causes or the physical results of stress.

10. Think Positively

Look for the good, not the bad. Some people approach each situation with the idea that a storm cloud crouches behind every silver lining instead of a silver lining waiting behind every cloud. They approach life with the idea that it's a half-empty glass when they could just as well view life as being a half-full glass. You'll help yourself if you will learn to major on what you have instead of what you don't have. You don't have to see life through rose-colored glasses but maybe you do need a clearer view. Maybe your view of the problems has blocked your seeing the resources available for dealing with those problems.

11. Cultivate a Sense of Humor

I heard about a fellow who methodically had kept track of how he spent his lifetime of eighty years. He calculated that he had spent twenty-one years at work, twenty-six years in bed, six years eating, five years waiting for others, six years being angry, and forty-six hours laughing. It seems to me he should have laughed a lot more than that.

Laughter is great medicine for a lot of things. "A merry heart doeth good like a medicine," according to the Book of Proverbs in the Bible.[19]

Laughter is a great way to reduce stress. Laughter is like a thunderstorm in your brain. You logically expected a certain conclusion to be drawn, but the punch line brought a conclusion you did not expect. Laughter reflects your brain's recognition of this fact. Laughter is the brain's expression of playful delight that you, smart as you are, have been tricked.[20]

Laughter helps you see life from a different perspective. So, you'll help yourself deal with stress if, in the midst of your serious busy-ness, you will let yourself see and experience another side of life—humor.

Personalizing This Idea

A spiritual leader from the past points out the problem folks sometimes have in dealing with stress. Thomas a' Kempis wrote, "All men love peace but few love those things which make for peace." We could paraphrase that saying like this to fit this chapter's idea about stress: *All people want to master the tension of stress but too few want to do the things that would accomplish such mastery.*

Be one of the few; put into practice at least one of these ways of dealing with stress. There's no sense blaming others for the stress you feel.

Your work setting may contain many negative factors that are causing stress in your life. You may be able to encourage your employer to make some changes that would help the situation.

Some stress-causing factors you will simply need to deal with yourself, however. As in the rest of this book, I've tried to deal in this chapter with some ways you can do something about those things in *your* control.

You may not have much control over your job situation, but you probably have more control than you think you do. Use what you have. Master the tension of stress in your life on the job and off. Do something about those areas over which you can exercise control, however limited you may feel they are, in order to reduce the stress you feel.

Key Points

1. Stress can be good or bad.
2. Sources of stress on the job: see the six suggested.
3. Review and practice the eleven ways to master stress.

Notes

1. Hans Selye, *The Stress of Life*, revised edition (New York: McGraw-Hill, 1976), 74.

2. Vernon E. Buck, *Working Under Pressure* (New York: Crane, Russak & Company, Inc., 1972), 161.

3. Ibid., 46.

4. Dr. George Stotelmyer Everly, Jr. and Dr. Daniel A. Girdano, *The Stress Mess Solution: The Causes and Cures of Stress on the Job* (Bowie, Md.: Robert J. Brady Co., A Prentice-Hall Company, 1980), 33.

5. Ibid., 44.

6. Studs Terkel, *Working: People Talk About What They Do All Day and How They Feel About What They Do* (New York: Pantheon Books, 1974), xxi-xxii.

7. Buck, *Working Under Pressure*, 48, citing Melville Dalton, *Men Who Manage* (New York: Wiley, 1959), 82.

8. Everly and Girdano, *The Stress Mess Solution*, 44.

9. Ibid., 35-36.

10. Ibid., 19-20.

11. Ibid., 80-81.

12. Alan Lakein, *How to Get Control of Your Time and Your Life* (New York: New American Library, 1973), 96.

13. Everly and Girdano, *The Stress Mess Solution*, 152.

14. Ibid., 24.

15. Rosalind Forbes, *Corporate Stress* (Garden City, N. Y.: Doubleday & Company, 1979), 34-35.

16. See, for example, Everly and Girdano, *The Stress Mess Solution*, 95-150. See also Wayne E. Oates, *Your Right to Rest*, Potentials: Guides to Productive Living (Philadelphia: The Westminster Press, 1984), 47-48.

17. Al Cadenhead, Jr., *Hurry Up and Rest* (Nashville, Tenn.: Broadman Press, 1988), 118, citing Joe Richardson, "The Christian and Stress" (Nashville: The Sunday School Board of the Southern Baptist Convention, 1975), 27.

18. Everly and Girdano, *The Stress Mess Solution*, 62.

19. Proverbs 17:22.

20. Karl Albrecht, *Brain Power: Learn to Improve Your Thinking Skills* (Englewood Cliffs, N. J.: Prentice-Hall, Inc., 1980), 37.

7
Get Organized

Not long ago a couple of would-be holdup men in a small town in Louisiana had what can only be described as a bad day. Their intentions were good, as robbers' intentions go. They intended to accomplish the following: (a) steal a truck; (b) rob a service station; (c) make a clean getaway; and (d) spend the money. Some problems developed, though.

The two fellows accomplished (a) and (b), much as they had intended. They (a) stole a truck and drove to the service station. They (b) held up the service station and got the money. They then got back in the truck with the money and roared off toward (c), intending to make a clean getaway.

Unbelievably, they journeyed only one-half mile toward (c) when the truck ran out of gas! When the two holdup men got out of the truck to try to figure out why it would not go anymore and what to do next, the police captured them and retrieved the money. Goal (d)—spend the money—was now out of the question.

Basically what we have here is an organizational problem. These two not-so-bright robbers simply failed to get organized.

Perhaps the two of them never decided who was supposed to check the gasoline in the truck they stole. Or maybe one of them was supposed to be filling up the truck at the self-service pump while the other was inside robbing the cash register. Maybe a day-old newspaper was in the truck, the man left behind got engrossed in the comics, and he just let that little task go. Maybe he felt putting in gasoline was unimportant; after all, how many trucks run out of gas during holdups? Maybe he was just in a bad mood that day. Maybe he wanted to drive and his partner wouldn't let him. Maybe he felt it wasn't fair that he had got stuck with putting gas in the truck.

Whatever the case, for want of a little bit of gasoline and luck, those two had a rather unhappy day at work. They probably have spent some unhappy days since, too, behind bars.

I confess I don't know exactly what happened to foil the plans of these fellows, but the incident itself *did* happen. I read it in the weekly newspaper from that town myself.

Whatever the details, I say again that the problem was a lack of organization. And a lack of organization can lead to a great deal of unhappiness in many situations, including your job. You can increase your happiness even in a job you sometimes can't stand if you will take action aimed at getting organized in your work.

Organize Your Work

Finding out what you are really supposed to be doing in your job is the beginning point for getting a handle on the matter of organization. Your job description, written or unwritten, is the first place to look for the answer. What did your company hire you to do? Clarifying that point is important. You may have some discretion in how you go about fulfilling your job description. Or what you are supposed to do and how you are supposed to do it may be rather clear-cut, with little room for considering alternate ways of accomplishing the job.

A second place to find the answer to what you are really supposed to be doing is the accumulation of specific assignments your supervisor has given you. Those specific assignments may be clarifications of what is in your job description, or they may fall under the category of "other duties as assigned." It's not unusual for "other duties as assigned" to be what your real job is, by the way.

When you have checked these two sources to discover what you are supposed to be doing on your job, the next step is to get the tasks into manageable size. Do you know how to eat an elephant? The answer: one bite at a time.

Likewise, breaking those big assignments down into manageable, understandable chunks is helpful, even necessary, in getting on top of your work and feeling good, or at least better, about it. A big assignment sometimes looks fearfully difficult, so much so that anxiety is our response. Breaking down the assignment into bite-sized pieces helps us to feel we know what we are doing and are capable of accomplishing the job. We not only feel we are doing a better job; most likely we *are* doing a better job.

You can manage almost any big task if you will find out how you can divide it into smaller tasks. You can then take these small tasks step-by-step until you have accomplished them all.

Organize Your Time

My wife claims she heard me talking in my sleep one night several years ago, and this is what she said I said, probably out of a stress-filled life: "I've got so many demands on my time." That's true for too many of us too much of the time. Maybe it's true for you.

The amount of time people have is identical, of course. No one gets more, or less, than 168 hours per week. What is *not* identical is the amount and kind of responsibilities people have and the skills they know and use in managing time. Here are some important skills you need if you have any discretion whatsoever in how you manage your time on the job.

1. Keep a Daily "To-Do" List

On one piece of paper, list the items you intend to do that day. List the large and the small things that need doing. Base this list on the two items we just identified—your written or unwritten job description and the accumulation of specific assignments your supervisor has given you that you have not yet completed. You might have a list of ten or fifteen things to do you think you need to do today. Of course, don't list the routine things that you are going to do, like switch on your typewriter or computer, unless that's something you've been forgetting to do and wondering why the thing won't work.

You may think keeping a list is a rather simple, mundane, unsophisticated thing to do. Maybe it is, but it works. There's something about putting on paper what you need to do that is an important organizational step toward getting the tasks done. Unless you're a member of Mensa, the organization for the super-intelligent, you need a list, and I'm told that some of those folks do better working from a list, too. So, make your to-do list. In fact, make a new to-do list each day.

2. Set Priorities for the Items on Your List

Put "A" beside the two or three most important tasks, "B" beside the next most important tasks, and "C" beside the least important tasks. Number the "A's" according to which you need to work on first, second, and so on. Then number the "B's" in the same manner. Don't worry about numbering the "C's." The "C's" will take care of themselves. When you have finished identifying the "A's," "B's," and "C's" and you have numbered the "A's" and "B's," beside each item will be a letter and a number like A-1, B-1, C.

How can you identify "A's"? Answering the following questions will help:

● *Who* asked you to do the particular task? Your supervisor? The task is an obvious "A." If your boss thinks a certain task is a priority task, that's obviously what you need to work on. If you value your job or your relationship with your supervisor, you will zero in on "A" tasks before you turn to the "B's" and "C's."

● *What* is the task? Is the task in line with the main thrust of your job? The most important tasks are the tasks that lead you to accomplish the big goals of your job.

If you are an editor, for example, it would seem that editing manuscripts would be more important than reading junk mail or newsletters from organizations of which you are a member. Reading such material might eventually be helpful, even necessary, but certainly could not be considered more important than doing the big thing in your job—editing.

● *When* is the task due? Today? Or is it a big task that is due two days from now but that will take all the time you have to do a good job? It's a definite "A."

So much for the "A's." What about the "B's"? The "B" tasks are those matters that seem pretty important but that don't quite rise to the "A" level. A "B" certainly is important; it certainly needs doing. But not before you complete the "A's."

The "C" tasks are those matters that don't have *your* name on them, don't have a date on them, and/or are repetitive—such as cleaning out your desk drawers or straightening your files. There may come a day when the desk drawers get so messy or the files get so out of order that their respective conditions interfere with your work. Then, and only then, would cleaning out the drawers or straightening the files be pushed to a "B" level.

Under extraordinary conditions, any "C" task may become an "A," in fact. Before you clean out your desk drawers or straighten your files, however, see my suggestion number 3 that follows.

Of course, any task you have labeled "C" could automatically and immediately become an "A" if circumstances occurred to warrant it. Let's say I have received an information sheet about some program or product I care little about. I look at it and see that it's a "C," no doubt about it. If the information sheet is brief, I might glance at it sometime when I'm on hold on the telephone, but probably not. Suppose, though, my boss comes in and says, "Did you get that information sheet from XYZ company? I want you to give me a report on that by tomorrow morning at nine o'clock." That "C" has zoomed to an "A-1." The fact is, though, that very few "C's" ever become anything but "C's." They live and die as "C's." They never have even fifteen minutes of being famous. And, when that rare "C" does get moved up to an "A," there generally is a tip-off of some sort that it is about to ascend to a position of greater importance.

Thus, the risk in treating a "C" as a "C" until you find out differently is absolutely worth it. Do a great job on the "A's" and the odds are much in your favor that nobody will ever question why you had to have a little time to complete the matter you thought was a "C." You can forget about most "C's," in fact.

Don't be too concerned whether something is a "B" or a "C." What you really are trying to do is identify the "A's" and give your priority to them. The payoffs in accomplishment and satisfaction come in doing "A's."

Do you recall the bank robber of the thirties who was asked why he robbed banks? He replied, "Because that's where the money is." When it comes to getting money, banks are "A's."

The moral of that immoral story is, find the "A's" in your job and do them. A time management expert has estimated that on a "to-do" list of ten items, two of them will yield eighty per cent of the results in reaching your goals.[1] Those two are "A's." Find these items and do them. That's where the payoff is.

A word of caution—identifying the "A's" is where you will face your greatest problems in organizing. "A's" generally are the hard jobs, the big jobs, the jobs that require large outlays of time and energy. The same time management expert suggests that one reason we avoid doing many "A's" is that they are so big and complex that we know we can't do them perfectly. We can sharpen a pencil pretty close to perfect, though. So we go for such a "C" task and avoid the "A."[2]

You've probably heard about the Procrastinators' Club of America. The story is they have only about 35,000 members officially, but they have half a million unofficially. The reason for the discrepancy between the official and the unofficial membership figure is simple. The 465,000 would-be members really want to be members but just keep putting it off!

Don't put off the "A's" yourself. That's where the payoff is.

3. Give Prime Time to Prime Tasks

Do prime tasks—the "A" tasks—when your energy and attention level are at their highest. Save "B's"—lesser tasks—for time when your powers of concentration have lessened and you have completed all the "A" items. Some "B's" and "C's"—like reading memos and bulletins—can be put in those cracks of time when you've been put on hold on the telephone or can't give your powers of concentration to an "A."

For example, in my work I try to limit all opening of mail and searching through my "In" box to the late afternoon, after I have completed the major projects—the "A's"—I had planned for that day. Thus, opening and answering first class mail would fit in the "B" group for me. I think the best use of my time at the beginning of the day is to start on the big "A" tasks. In the afternoon, when I review my "In" box, a first-class letter becomes a "B" task unless an "A"—a report to my supervisor, for example—is pressing me. I include in "C" such things as brochures, information sheets, surveys—items that won't matter very much at all whether I as one lone individual deal with them or not. If something doesn't have my very own name on it, together with a due date, it's automatically a "C," and a low one at that, until I find out differently.

4. Complete the "A's" Before You Move on to the "B's"

Keep working on the "A" items until you complete them all. Resist every impulse to flee to a "C" or even a "B" until you have completed the "A's," unless extraordinary circumstances develop—such as your supervisor assigning you an item you had considered a "C."

5. When You Complete an Item, Cross It Off or Check It

Each such mark is a mark of accomplishment about which you can feel good. Even when you're not the happiest you can be in your job, you can at least celebrate *your* accomplishments.

Organize Your Workplace

You may feel that I am treading on your personality when I suggest that organizing your workplace is important. You may protest that you are just not a neat person. Let me assure you that organization, not neatness, is the issue here, though I do think there is some relationship between the two matters.

A high school teacher of mine insisted that his students put this motto on the notebook we kept during the year: "Neatness is a mark of character." Well, that may or may not be so. I suppose some pretty unscrupulous, immoral folks are neat. Nevertheless, a certain level of orderliness does say something about how efficiently and effectively most people can function on the job.

I'm not really concerned with whether your filing and storage system and your workplace look exceptionally neat. You do need to be able to do your work without spending time looking through piles of stuff for an item you need, however. Organizing your workplace calls for having a place for tools, equipment, and other paraphernalia of your job and for keeping such items where you can find them without turning the world upside down. Having "a place for everything and everything in its place" will assist most folks in being more efficient and more effective in their jobs.

Some folks seem to be able to function with debris all around them better than others can. I'm not the kind of neatness freak than insists on having only one piece of paper on my desk at a time. (If you are, that's okay by me, and I take back the word "freak." You are a little unusual, though.) However, confidence in managing my work calls for me to have no more than two small stacks of stuff and to know what is in those stacks. When the stacks get too high and too many, and when I cannot readily recall what is in those tasks, it seems to me that I can hear the faint ticks of time bombs coming from the direction of those stacks.

You need to find the level of orderliness and neatness at which you can function best. Then, organize your workplace accordingly. Try to strike a balance between being compulsive about neatness and being a slob whose work area is almost indistinguishable from the garbage can.

Organize Your Self

To get organized on the job, you need to organize your work, organize your time, and organize your workplace. But these matters won't do all the good they can toward bringing organization to reality unless you do something about organizing your *self*. Organizing your *self* means (1) organizing your *attitudes* toward your job and, indeed, toward all of life and (2) organizing your *actions*.

Organizing Your Attitudes Toward Your Job

I speculated in the first few paragraphs of this chapter that one reason the would-be robbers of the gasoline station failed could have been a poor attitude on the part of the fellow who was supposed to have filled up the stolen truck with gasoline. The idea is far-fetched, I know. But it's not far-fetched to acknowledge that people do sabotage themselves in their jobs because of poor attitudes.

People certainly do stifle their *enjoyment* of their jobs by poor attitudes. By "poor" attitudes, I mean negative attitudes. You can help to organize *your* self on the job and off by developing a more positive attitude.

The idea of positive thinking is either affirmed or belittled, depending on which crowd of experts you listen to. Some folks put positive thinking in the category of fantasy or self-hypnosis. Such is hardly the case, in my opinion.

The simple truth is that we choose our perspective on life. Teaching yourself to think positively is simply exercising your choice about how you will view life in general and your life in particular.

You can look at life, including your job, negatively, or you can look at your life and your job positively. It's your choice. As you make the choice, be aware that positive thinking produces positive results, while negative thinking produces negative results. You do want positive results, don't you?

Humor me a little. Think with me positively just a bit about positive thinking. What is positive thinking? Positive thinking is focusing your attention on the positive side of a subject.[3] Hans Selye, the pioneer researcher on stress, found this idea about positive thinking in the words of a piece of folk advice he learned as a child:

> Imitate the Sundial's Ways
> Count Only the Pleasant Days.[4]

Positive thinking is not just focusing your attention on the positive side of a subject, however. Positive thinking also calls for expressing one's thoughts about that subject by using positive language.[5]

Our words *express* our thoughts and feelings, but our words also *affect* our thoughts and feelings. Thus, by talking about positive aspects of a subject you will be more likely to experience positive thoughts and feelings about it. Apply this concept to your attitude toward your job. If you can get yourself to focus on the positive aspects of your job and to talk about those positive aspects rather than focusing on and talking about the negative, you will increase your positive feelings about your job or any part of that job.[6] Is that cheating? I think it's smart.

You can see and talk about your job as being a bunch of rainy days interspersed with some days of sunshine. Or you can see and talk about your job as being a bunch of days of sunshine interspersed with some rainy days. You can mark all the rainy days on your calendar, or you can mark all the sunny days. You can focus your thoughts and your words on the problems, or you can focus your thoughts and your words on solutions to the problems.

So, do yourself a favor, organize your attitudes—your *self*—to focus on the positive. Why make yourself and others miserable by focusing on the negative?

An office worker's job included what for her was a very boring task. On several days each month she had to fill in figures and statistics in various forms. The work was routine in the worst kind of way. She resolved, however, that she would find a way to make it interesting.

On those days when she had to fill in the forms, she played a game with herself as she did the work. She kept track of the number of forms she filled in each morning and tried to beat that number in the afternoon. The next day, she tried to beat the total for the day before.

She didn't get a raise, a promotion, or praise for her efforts. What she did get, though, was a greater sense of fulfillment and accomplishment. She was able to get more joy out of a dull assignment.[7] Her attitude made the difference. She could not control the assignment of that boring task. She could, though, control how she performed that task. By making a game of it, she turned it into play.

Organizing Your Actions on the Job

A few years ago, an automobile rental company used the slogan, "We try harder." Of course, results, not trying harder, are what is important. There is something to be said, nevertheless, for the discipline of giving your best to the job. The best results are not likely to come without the discipline of trying hard by giving your best to the job.

Organizing your actions at work toward the discipline of giving your best is important and noteworthy, especially in light of the approach too many fellow workers seem to take to their work. A college professor tells of a teacher of his who facetiously rewrote the Ten Commandments to reflect the "just-enough-to-get-by" attitude of too many Americans. The revised first commandment went like this: "I am the Lord thy God who brought thee out of the house of the European tyrants into my own land, America: Relax!"[8]

Discipline, however, leads to competence on the job. Competence on the job leads to a measure of inner satisfaction, even when the job is not all you might wish it to be.[9] If you are looking for a soft spot, you might try feeling the top of your head. Feeling the top of your head won't make you happier on the job, but the top of your head is the only sure place to find a soft spot. A disciplined approach to your job is a necessity.

Personalizing This Idea

A visitor to the swamps and bayous of south Louisiana met a grizzled Cajun hunter. The visitor noticed that the Cajun was wearing an unusual necklace and commented on it. In his heavy accent, the Cajun explained that the necklace was made out of alligator teeth.

Ignorant of the ways of the swamps, the visitor said, "Oh, I see. That's like someone from another part of the country wearing a string of pearls then, isn't it?" The Cajun replied, "I guess so, but anybody can open an oyster."

The Cajun was saying that one's view of his work depended on whether one considered it to be like opening an oyster's shell or opening an alligator's mouth. In which category does your job fit? Whatever the case, organization is required to get the job done.

Considerably more organization would seem to be required for the alligator-like jobs. On the hunch that you probably consider your job to be one of those alligator-type jobs, I encourage you to recognize that there's no substitute for organization—of your work, your time, your workplace, and, yes, yourself—if you want to be happier in your work.

Key Points

1. Organize your work.
2. Organize your time.
   Review the five suggestions for organizing your time.
3. Organize your workplace.
4. Organize your self.

Notes

1. Alan Lakein, *How to Get Control of Your Time and Your Life* (New

York: New American Library, 1973), 71.

2. Ibid., 69.

3. Karl Albrecht, *Brain Power: Learn to Improve Your Thinking Skills* (Englewood Cliffs, N. J.: Prentice-Hall, Inc., 1980), 90.

4. Hans Selye, *The Stress of Life*, revised edition (New York: McGraw-Hill Book Co., 1976), 418.

5. Albrecht, 90.

6. Ibid., 91-92.

7. Dale Carnegie, *How to Enjoy Your Life and Your Job* (New York: Pocket Books, 1985), 39-40.

8. Allan Bloom, *The Closing of the American Mind* (New York: Simon and Schuster, 1987), 227.

9. See Frederick Herzberg, *Work and the Nature of Man* (Cleveland: The World Publishing Company, 1966), 95-96.

8
Decide to Grow

A few years ago I visited the Queen Mary—the ship, you know. This great ocean liner once sailed the seas of the world. Now it is permanently moored at Long Beach, California, near Los Angeles. The ship attracts many tourists, and it's worth seeing, in my opinion.

The tour of the ship includes a documentary movie that tells the story of the ship's majestic past. With a flourish of triumphant music, the movie ends with this line: "The greatest ship that ever went to sea is now the greatest ship to come and see."

I'm sure that sentence was intended to impress the viewers with the grandeur of the opportunity to tour such a ship. The sentence depresses as well as uplifts. True, the sentence speaks of a glorious past. The ship was involved in exciting events in both peace and war. The sentence speaks also, however, of a present that is not nearly so exciting. The Queen Mary is safe in the harbor, but ships are not built to be safe in harbors. They are built to travel the seas to distant ports.

About the worst thing you can do when you are not as happy in your job as you want to be is to seek a safe hiding place, curl up in the fetal position, and hope no one finds you. Instead of avoiding life, it's time to take some initiative. It's time to seek ways to grow in competence in your present job as well as broaden your horizons for whatever the future may hold.

Staying where you are, as you are, is not the right approach for dealing with unhappiness on the job. "The saddest people I know," said the president of one of the largest chains of newspapers in the United States, "are those who have spent thirty or forty years working for the same employer doing something they *almost* like."[1]

Does this mean you need to get busy sending out resumes and setting up job interviews? Not necessarily. At least finish reading this book and put the ideas into practice for a while before you do that! Instead of searching for another job, you may get help by finding ways to grow in the skills and outlook that would increase your competence in your present job. Increased happiness often comes as a by-product of growth. So . . .

Take Stock of Yourself

The need to learn continues throughout life. Read that sentence again, please. What do you think about it?

You may consider that sentence a threat if your experience in formal education was more or less unhappy. You may consider it threatening, too, if you already have invested years and years of your life—not to mention of your money—in formal education. Maybe you thought you were through with learning. The idea of continuing to learn may be troubling, too, if you just don't see how you can spare any energy, time, or money, right now to get more education.

Don't push aside the need to continue to learn, though. Finding ways to grow by learning will likely cost you something, but your unhappiness with your job is costing you something, too, isn't it? If nothing else, your lack of happiness with your job is costing you peace of mind and a sense of fulfillment. They're worth a lot. Continuing to learn is important.

Not only does the *need* to learn continue throughout life,

but the *opportunity* to learn continues also. You weren't through learning when you completed whatever formal education you've received. The opportunity to learn is larger than a box that comprises the first third or so of our lives.[2] We can get out of that box and keep on learning all of our lives. Further, we *must* get out of that box and keep on learning if we are to live in the most joyful and productive manner.

Assuming you're willing to accept your need to keep on learning, then you're ready to begin to take stock of what you need to learn. As you do this, you're asking the question, *What do I really need to learn?*

Some adults, unfortunately, don't have much experience answering this question. They have referred to others this question of what they need to learn. They have taken others' answers all their lives. They have accepted the mistaken idea that they should simply take what others want to give them rather than identifying themselves the needs they have.

One of the hallmarks of being a mature adult, however, is that adults accept responsibility for their lives. A lot of the ideas in this book relate to just that. Taking responsibility for your own life includes taking responsibility for your educational life.

What do I really need to learn? It's really your question to answer. You can shove it off to someone else. You can let someone else decide for you, but that person's decision may or may not be the right decision for you.

Adults who want to grow by learning need to see themselves as consumers with a range of choices for their educational investment of dollars, time, and energy. That's why it's important for you to answer carefully the question, *What do I really need to learn?*

How can you find out what you really need to learn? Consider these varied possibilities for clues:

(1) The most important source for finding out what you really need to learn is yourself and your achievements. Take some time to take stock of yourself—who you are, what you value, what you enjoy, what you have achieved, and, most important, what you have *enjoyed achieving.* Focus on the things you have achieved—not necessarily the things for which you have received medals but the things that come to mind that identify for you the things in which you feel you have succeeded and which you have enjoyed doing the most.[3]

As you engage in this exercise, the goal is to identify the areas of your greatest strengths and improve even further on those strengths. Why? A couple of reasons:

• First, the payoff for building on your strengths is greater than the payoff for getting a little better at the things you're weak in. You may be able to become an expert in the areas of your strengths. People who are great in skills that are worthwhile and needed are in demand. As career counselor Bernard Haldane suggests, "The right combination of your skills is what makes you valuable to your employer and 'alive' to your friends and family."[4] The payoff is more than doubled if you enjoy using these skills, too.

• Second, the frustrations are less when you build on your strengths than when you try to get a little better in the areas of your weakness. Overcoming your weaknesses may be valuable and should not be ignored completely, but improving in your areas of weakness may be considerably more time-consuming and frustrating than building on your strengths.[5]

(2) Here's another source for finding out what you need to learn. Think of the people who are the best in your particular line of work. What do these people know that you don't know? What do they do well that you have some abilities in yourself that you could develop further?

(3) Think of times when you have felt inadequate in per-

forming your work. What knowledge and skills would have enabled you to feel more confident? Are these the kinds of knowledge and skills you would like to develop? Can you think of yourself as feeling good about having such knowledge and skills?

(4) Think of new equipment and new processes that would improve the way you function in doing your job. How can you learn how to use such equipment and processes?

(5) As you look for clues in these areas, consider gathering information from other people, too. Talk to fellow workers in the same jobs. Talk with your supervisor.

(6) Consider the published information that relates to your job, especially if it comes from recognized organizations or known veterans of the work. Such information is the accumulated wisdom of trailblazers, veterans who know the ropes. You would be wise to learn from them.

Make a list of the clues you get from these sources and others you might think of yourself. This list of your needs is essential as you chart your own path of growth. Next you need to . . .

Take Stock of the Opportunities

The first question is, *What do I really need to learn?* The second question is, *Where can I learn what I really need to learn?*

You may think that the first and most important answer to this question is, *take a course* or *earn a degree.* As a matter of fact, that may well be the answer. So don't shut the door on the possibility too soon. It's not necessarily the answer, however.

What you have identified that you really need to learn may not be available in a course or a degree. So, let's look at the varied range of possibilities for growing in the knowledge, skills, and attitudes that you feel you need to develop.

Talk to Other People

In almost any occupation, people must learn some very important matters from fellow workers. These fellow workers simply have information or skills that others don't yet have, and they are willing to share them. In your drive toward growth in learning, don't neglect the informal learning opportunities of personal contact with fellow workers.

Maybe professional computer operators learn all they need to know in a school of some sort. Nevertheless, we amateurs who use personal computers in our work find ourselves learning much from one another.

In fact, when our company installed a network of computers recently, people learned most through informal conversations with other people who knew just a little bit more than they did. As people discovered new processes, they shared their new ideas with others. The electronic grapevine worked in a most efficient manner. Although formal courses were offered, the day-to-day learning really made the greatest difference.

Read Manuals, Books, and Articles

How much easier life would be if we would all learn to read the directions first! A wealth of learning is available in those marvelously portable teaching machines called books. In seeking to develop your knowledge, skills, and attitudes, don't neglect the printed material that relates to your work. Included are such mundane matters as the manuals for the machines you operate and how-to materials on specific details of your work. You can proceed from there to the books that exist on almost every aspect of every occupation. A planned personal reading program can enhance almost anyone's work and contribute to the enjoyment of that work.

Limitations exist, of course. Nobody wants a brain surgeon who learned everything he or she knows by reading self-help books and do-it-yourself manuals. Some subjects can't be mastered just by reading books.

Reading can contribute to mastering many subjects, though. Before this chapter is over, you'll be considering possible sources of learning that will match your current circumstances. Learning through reading is a possibility for almost everyone.

Learn from Audio and Video Tapes

A great deal of helpful information is available on audio and video tapes. You may commute to work in a car, or you may jog or walk in your spare time. You could capitalize on that time by investing in an inexpensive audiocassette player and using the time to learn about subjects that are important to you.

Some such tapes may be available through your company or through the local public library. Be cautious about investing a lot of money in buying tapes yourself, though, unless you are prepared to invest a similar amount of time and personal energy. Unless you have unlimited financial resources, investigate the availability of free material. Beware of media come-ons, at least until you know what's available for free. You won't listen to even the best tapes more than a few times most likely. Thus, investing a lot of money in tapes doesn't seem wise, unless you're sure they're that important and are not available without charge.

Attend Workshops and Seminars

Your company may offer free workshops and seminars related to your work. Resolve now to take them, as many as you can. Someone in your company must consider these workshops and seminars to be important and beneficial. Take advantage of the opportunities offered.

I hope you learn a great deal from these workshops. You likely will. An added plus is that your participation will demonstrate to others your desire to grow through learning. That's a good reputation to have, even if some such courses seem not as valuable or as interesting as you would like.

Participate in Workshops Offered by Your Professional Organization, If One Exists

Some organizations related to various occupations offer seminars to benefit their members. If you're serious about growing, you need to become a member of your professional organization and take advantage of the educational opportunities it offers. These kinds of training opportunities are often closely related to the real-life work world of that occupation.

Take Correspondence Courses

Reputable correspondence courses on many worthwhile subjects are available through accredited institutions, including universities. If you can't go to the institution, the institution can come to you by mail.

In some localities, the institution can come to you by means of television, too. Check out the offerings of the local educational television station or a nearby college for the possibility of such courses being available to you.

Be cautious, though, before shelling out money or investing your time in correspondence courses. Such courses can offer much to the learner. Be certain, however, that the institution is reputable and preferably accredited. At least be sure that the course aims to accomplish the goal you have set for yourself.

Attend Accredited Vocational Institutes

Some institutes offer evening and weekend classes that might fit your work schedule. Some companies pay for such training when employees express interest and meet certain standards.

Participate in College and Professional Programs

All kinds of folks go to college. Some are young; some are not-so-young. Changing economic situations, plant closings, plus the great desire of adults for learning opportunities have resulted in college classrooms being populated by folks of all ages, including older adults.

You supply the definition of "older adults." The age range at many colleges is wide. And, you'll never be any younger than you are right now. Don't let age be the excuse that keeps you from growing.

Some adults go to college early in the morning or late in the evening, before or after a day's work. Some attend school on weekends. Some work on undergraduate degrees, some on graduate degrees, some on professional degrees.

Many colleges recognize that their market is not just the teenager fresh out of high school. Instead, their market includes the adult who is ten, twenty, thirty, or more years out of high school, the adult who is seeking to begin or finish that degree he or she never had a chance to earn. Or the college market is the mid-career adult who is seeking to hone his or her skills or pick up an additional skill that did not even exist a few years earlier.

College might be the place you should go to learn the knowledge and skills you've identified as your need. If that's what you discover, you won't be the only adult there. Investigation might reveal, too, that area colleges have made provisions for adults with your needs.

Again, be cautious in choosing a course of study, even at colleges. Will it really meet your needs? Will the result be worth the investment of your time, energy, and money?

You need to investigate carefully by talking to the folks in your community who are in a position to evaluate the value of courses and degrees from a particular college. School counselors and other people you trust can be of help. Don't neglect alumni of this institution and this particular course. Are they satisfied customers? Next . . .

Match Needs and Opportunities

The first question is, *What do I really need to learn?* The second question is, *Where can I learn what I really need to learn?* The third question is, *Which of these sources of learning best meet my needs and are appropriate to my budgets?*

"Budgets"—plural—is the right word in that third question. Many budgets come into play in your life. You will need to take them all into account as you try to match your learning needs to the right sources of learning.

Consider first the *monetary budget.* Some of the sources of learning available to you do cost money in greater or lesser amounts. Some sources—like college—cost a lot of money, in fact. You will need to evaluate your own monetary budget to determine whether you believe the amount is worth the expected result.

My own experience verifies that education is always worthwhile. What you're trying to do is find the best education value for the dollar.

If money is a problem (and for whom is it not?), then I encourage you to take advantage of all the free or nearly free learning opportunities that meet your learning needs. Don't assume, however, that those learning opportunities that cost a good bit of money are automatically out of reach for you. Perhaps money is available from your company for employee training. Perhaps scholarships are available from the school or from other sources. Perhaps you need to re-order your expense priorities for something truly important and meaningful to you for a lifetime.

Almost everything worthwhile costs. Delete that word *almost.* Everything worthwhile *does* cost in some way or other. So, don't be surprised that the valuable commodity of education costs. Most are willing to pay for the things they think are worthwhile.

Some advisers suggest that people might do well to earmark one percent of their annual income for personal development in the knowledge, skills, and attitudes of the jobs they do—or would like to prepare to do. Some courses of study will cost more than that one percent, of course—a lot more. But the cost of such achievements as a college or professional degree should be figured over a lifetime of work and not simply over the time of study itself. The satisfaction that comes from self-assured competence is worth a lot, too.

In choosing the best learning sources for your needs, you must consider your *time and energy budget*, too. Some folks can function well when they are doing a lot of different things. Others can't. Some folks have no problem being pleasant and productive when every waking moment is committed to something. Others do. Some folks have lots of obligations to care for already besides work, like responsibilities as a mother or father of little children.

Your other life obligations may not leave a lot of time and energy for educational development. You may not be able to function well with a packed calendar and an insistent clock. If so, you have some decisions to make. What can you let go for a time in order to devote some time to personal development? Can you get others to share the load with you for a while?

Or/and, maybe you should consider taking a steady, deliberate pace toward personal development rather than trying to run on the fast track. Better to go more slowly and succeed, in my opinion, than to run headlong toward the goal and falter before finishing. A slower trip is a lot better than no trip at all.

I know a married couple right now who have been in school, one or the other or both of them, since I first met them. That was more than ten years ago. When I first met the husband, he had no college degree. He's now close to earning a doctorate. When I first met the wife, she was about halfway through completing a college degree. Now she's close to earning a doctorate, too.

Ten years ago this couple could have reasoned that their educational dreams were too high and that they would never achieve them. They could have given up even before they started. They've taken a slower route, and they've done without some of the material things lots of folks think are important. Learning is important to them.

Another friend earned a law degree at night. Taking this route required about twice the amount of time as usual. He's now a successful attorney, however.

None of these three friends would say it was or is easy. They demonstrate, however, that it can be done, at least by some folks, if they're willing to pay the price from their various budgets. Maybe by you, if that's your thing.

However you need to balance your various budgets, don't give up or put off the important matter of personal development. Your educational quest may be a long-distance run rather than a hundred-yard dash. Don't worry about that. Just get started and do the best you can with the money, time, and energy that you have or can acquire.

Personal growth can enrich your life and put more happiness into your job situation. Now is the time to get started.

Personalizing This Idea

Growth is risky business. People are often afraid of risks. Indeed, some caution is both understandable and wise. Still, risks are necessary. We must learn to face and deal with risks, including the risks of growth.

A person can be too cautious, especially about trying to learn new things. Generally speaking, wouldn't you say that ignorance is a lot riskier than knowledge?

It's true that a little learning is a dangerous thing, as wise Ben Franklin is supposed to have said. Remember that a little ignorance is pretty dangerous, too. Moreover, a lot of ignorance can be absolutely catastrophic. The world of work is no exception to the dangers of ignorance. It's dangerous to stop learning how to do your job better. It's personally satisfying to keep on learning. The chances are good that you can increase your joy in your work by deciding to grow. Such a decision will likely move you out of your comfort zone, at least for a while. Growing takes effort and calls for at least some risk.

Apathy and stagnation don't contribute to happiness. Growth does. Decide to grow in the areas that are important to you. It's worth it.

Key Points

1. Take stock of yourself.
   Check back on the six things that help you find what you really need to learn about yourself and your job.
2. Take stock of the opportunities.
   Do you remember the eight opportunities? If not, review them.
3. Match needs and opportunities.

Notes

1. Walter Anderson, *Courage Is a Three-Letter Word* (New York: Fawcett Crest, 1986), 163-164. The italicized word is in the original.
2. See Richard Nelson Bolles, *The Three Boxes of Life* (Berkeley, Calif.: Ten Speed Press, 1981).
3. Helpful exercises that can lead you along step by step in identifying areas of personal achievement and enjoyment can be found in such sources as these:
   Richard Nelson Bolles, *The Three Boxes of Life* (Berkeley, Calif.: Ten Speed Press, 1981).
   Richard Nelson Bolles, *What Color Is Your Parachute? A Practical*

Manual for Job-Hunters & Career Changers (Berkeley, Calif.: Ten Speed Press, 1990). (Published annually.)

Bernard Haldane, *Career Satisfaction and Success: A Guide to Job Freedom* (New York: AMACOM, 1974).

4. Haldane, *Career Satisfaction and Success: A Guide to Job Freedom*, 34.

5. Richard Germann, Diane Blumenson, and Peter Arnold, *Working and Liking It* (New York: Fawcett Gold Medal, 1984), 8.

9
Live with Balance

It was Monday, 6 o'clock in the evening, time for supper (or dinner—whatever you call the evening meal at your house). The four-year-old stared at the rather full plate of lasagna in front of him. He liked lasagna, and from past experience, he knew this was going to be good lasagna.

He looked at his full plate and then at the serving dish. There was a lot of lasagna in that serving dish—enough to last two adults and a four-year-old for several meals. We're talking lots of lasagna—good lasagna, and lots of it. Sounds wonderful to some of us.

The four-year-old's mother had been busy for several days, getting ready to teach a summer children's program. Thus, this meal was the second in a row at which she had served lasagna. Remember, it was good lasagna, yes, but still, it was, again, lasagna. And there was a *lot* of lasagna.

The four-year-old looked at his full plate of lasagna and then surveyed the still-almost-full serving dish of lasagna. He calculated the situation. Good lasagna, and a lot of good lasagna, yes. But the perceptive four-year-old seemed to behold a week of lasagna staring him in the face that Monday evening. With quiet firmness, he announced to his mom that Monday evening, "I'll eat this lasagna today and tomorrow. But I'm not eating it next Friday."

Maybe you know how he felt. Even though lasagna might be your favorite food, you probably don't want to eat lasagna—or whatever your favorite food is, even prime rib, fried chicken, or lobster—every meal, day in and day out.

We crave variety, not sameness. Most of us want some degree of variety in the activities of our lives. Sleeping may be a favorite activity of yours, but it's unlikely you want to sleep twenty-four hours a day. The same thought holds for any of the activities in which we might engage. However much we enjoy *any* activity, we wouldn't want to do it *all* the time, every hour and minute of every day.

The point is this: balance is important in all of life, not just in the foods we choose. Achieving balance is certainly important in being happy in the job you sometimes can't stand.

Balance Work and Other Activities

More than a few folks have put all their eggs of happiness in one basket—their work. Perhaps the cultural conditioning of men leaves them especially vulnerable to this problem. Women, however, are gaining on men in this area. This over-investment in work by women and men is questionable progress. Just as we wouldn't be happy eating lasagna every meal (even *great* lasagna), we will hinder our happiness in our jobs if all we do is work. Expecting your job alone to provide fullness of satisfaction in life is a mistake.

People come nearer to enjoying their work when they engage in other activities besides work. Like what? Like rest and play and family and other people and hobbies. Like helping others and worshiping and learning and taking walks and looking at the clouds and the flowers. Like occasionally doing absolutely nothing.

One thing I enjoy about the seashore is the rhythmic motion of the waves rolling in and then receding. The waves roll in, and then they slide out. There's a balanced, rhythmic pattern to it all. What if the waves only rolled in and never slid out? It just wouldn't be the same, to say the least.

As with the waves, there's a time to go to work and a time to leave work behind for other pursuits. Failing to participate in this balanced rhythm of life may lead eventually to a measure of unhappiness even in a job you may love, not to mention the job you sometimes can't stand.

If just about all you are doing is working, no wonder you are not as happy in your work as you would like to be. It's time to take a fresh look at your priorities in life—not just in your job. And it's time to take a close look at the reasons for your drivenness about work.

If all you do is work, why? Why do you just work all the time? The matter of motivation is a key element in identifying who's a workaholic and who's drawn to his work and works long hours at it out of sheer delight. Workaholics often are motivated by fear, certainly a far cry from delight.[1]

So, start with some basic questions about your own over-emphasis on work. Whom or what do you fear? Do you fear the disapproval of someone who is important to you? Do you fear being demoted? Do you fear losing your job? Is your fear justified, justified enough to explain your out-of-balance work life? Do you need to confront that fear and take control of your part in the situation?

What do you hope to gain by your addiction to work? Approval from someone? A promotion? More and more money? Security? Are these matters for which you are trading your time, energy, and physical, mental, and spiritual well-being worth it? Do you consider the promotion, the prestige, the power, the extra money, and even the security to be adequate compensation for the price you may be paying in personal unhappiness or the unhappiness of others because of your misspent time? What are you trying to avoid? An unhappy home life? Loneliness?

Whatever reason you give for your over-emphasis on work, ask yourself another question. Is work solving your problem or creating more difficulty because you are avoiding the issue? Is your over-emphasis on work solving the problem in the short run while storing up sticks of dynamite for a major blow-up later on when the slightest spark will ignite them?

You may say that you aren't really addicted to work—that you're certainly not a workaholic; that you just have a lot to do right now. Ha, ha, ha. That's a good one. Forgive me for laughing at your feeble protest. I laugh because your protest reminds me of what I used to say about myself. Further, that excuse ("I'm not really a workaholic; I just have a lot to do right now.") is exactly what one of my well-meaning but very unperceptive workaholic friends kept telling me about himself and his workaholism for several years. "I'm not a workaholic; I just have a lot to do right now," he kept saying. Is that what you are saying? Pardon me, but I have personal experience with that excuse for an out-of-balance life. I've even used it myself.

You may think I am being too hard on you at this point. Perhaps I am. I certainly do not know your particular situation. Sometimes people do work long hours for reasons other than that they are workaholics. You may be new on the job, trying desperately to master it, or just hold onto it. You may thus find yourself working much longer hours than you wish. Or perhaps a special short-term project just needs to be completed and you have been elected to do the honors. Perhaps you really do need—not just want—the money for a worthy purpose.

Okay, any of that sounds reasonable. If one of those situations is yours, maybe your over-emphasis on work is justified right now. You need to watch yourself, though. These short-term, somewhat excusable, situations can be the beginnings of a pattern that lead you to over-value your work and neglect interests at least as important.[2] So, okay, but be careful, you hear?

On the other hand, if this excessive time at work has been

going on for months and especially years, or if it is just another event in a rather lengthy series of over-investments in work time, you may be trying to fool yourself. Maybe you're really not telling the truth to yourself about why you are working excessively. Maybe the money is for your wants after all, not your needs. Maybe you're really working on another agenda, not just trying to learn your job. Maybe you've got a sign on your back that says, "Overload me with work. I love it when I can tell others my back is breaking."

If such evaluations as these strike a personal nerve, then it's time to get honest with yourself and do something about the problem. Your work and life happiness may depend on your willingness to do just that.

Let me remind you that one doesn't have to *like* something to be addicted to it. If you find your life being dominated by your work, for whatever reason, it's time to take a close look at yourself and your priorities. Something's not right, and you need to take whatever control you can to remedy the situation.

As business consultants Waitley and Witt observe, "People who have the full joy of working get together with loved ones, their friends and neighbors. They love their careers but are not married to them. They care about performance, productivity, and profit, but also effectiveness, fairness, and honesty."[3] Balancing work and other activities is important to your happiness.

God has built into nature itself an intention for balance and rhythm. Read the first chapter of the Book of Genesis and you will see this truth. God worked, but even God turned His attention to other activities. Even God didn't work all the time.

So, if you are claiming divine sanction for your over-emphasis on work, forget it. Even God balanced work with rest.

A friend confronted someone in religious work who was working so hard that he never took a vacation. The right reverend workaholic piously replied, "The devil doesn't take a vacation." The sensible friend replied, "That's why the devil acts like the devil!" Could that be why you're at least feeling like the devil, if not acting that way? Since God rested, we would do well to learn from His example and do the same.

This divine example of balance provides a clue for human beings. Living with balance is one way human beings cooperate with, rather than go against, this rhythm that is built into nature itself. Life works best when we attune ourselves to this rhythm.

Dr. Wayne Oates, Professor of Psychiatry and Behavioral Sciences at the University of Louisville School of Medicine, tells of talking with a man about forty years old whom he found in a tuberculosis sanatorium. The man talked openly with Dr. Oates, who at that time was pastor of a church in Louisville.

From his hospital bed, the man reflected on his experience. He said he felt he was being paid back for his sin.

Professor Oates asked what he had done. The man replied, "I wanted it all."

Oates asked what he meant. The man explained that he had gotten a job at a local munitions plant. The pay was the most money he had ever made. "'I wanted it all. I would work three days three shifts without sleeping. Many days I would work two shifts. I was so greedy that I broke my health down and landed in here. That was my sin."[4]

You may or may not subscribe to the man's diagnosis that the root of his problem was his sin of greed. Too, you may feel that the attention you give to work is not nearly so out of balance as his seems to have been. The point, though, is that we open ourselves to difficulties of many sorts when we permit our lives to get out of balance.

Some machines—a washing machine, for example—won't work when they are out of balance. Human beings are more fearfully and wonderfully made than the finest machines.

Both work and other activities—including rest and relationships—are important. You think you are the exception to this intended balance and know better than God so that you do not need to give attention to this matter? Not likely.

Balance Other Activities and Work

Including in your life, in a balanced manner, other activities besides work can contribute to your happiness with your job. Like two sides of a see-saw, though, it's also important to learn to balance the other activities in your life with your work. What we do with our time, energy, and focus of attention outside of work can influence greatly the sense of well-being we have when we are at work.

A measure of work unhappiness may come from a person's life off the job, not from the job itself. Consider what individual workers may bring with them to work on a given day: the frustrations of snarled traffic, the latest angry encounter with a family member, the burden of caring for children or aging parents, the trauma of coping with teenagers, the stress of a crowded schedule of outside-of-work projects, the nagging load of health difficulties. The list is as varied as the human race.

In some cases, the job is a convenient scapegoat for our feelings of frustration, despair, anger, and depression because of what is happening to us outside of work. At least, a part of whatever degree of unhappiness people may experience on the job may be rooted in their lives away from work.

How can you balance work and these outside-of-work activities so as to result in greater happiness?

● First, recognize how your work happiness or lack thereof may be affected by your non-work activities.

● Second, apply the underlying principle of this book. That is, take control of whatever part of what is happening to you that you can take control of.

For example, outside-of-work hobbies or events may be sapping your physical and emotional energy so that you have little left to give to your job. The next step is lowered interest in your job and declining achievement on the job. The worst-case scenario may be that others, such as your supervisor, notice your work slipping and call that to your attention, to put it mildly perhaps. The consequence then is unhappiness on the job. Achieving greater happiness will call for achieving a healthier balance between your off-work and at-work life. In this case, the specific application means cutting back on your off-work life if you're serious about being happier on the job.

Sometimes we simply undertake too much for the time available. An anonymous proverb tells in three words the story of too many people in our society today. The sad tale goes like this: "Hurry, worry, bury."

We let our lives get out of rhythm and adopt a rush-rush pattern. There's no rhythm, no balance, just an endless pattern. As a wise counselor suggests, "We feel that life is passing us by when in fact we are passing life by in our pell-mell rush."[5]

You may feel trapped—even actually *be* trapped by circumstances that seem beyond your control—into such a rush-rush pattern of life. If so, look around in those circumstances for handles to grab to enable you to take whatever control you can. Maybe you are caring for an aging parent who requires much attention. Or perhaps a troubled teenager is a constant drain on your life. Whatever the case, catch whatever snatches of rest and relaxation, down-time and depressurization, that you can. Do whatever you can to bring some balance into your life.

And, resist the temptation to blame your unhappy feelings on your job, at least not all of these unhappy feelings. Don't complicate your life further by letting yourself feel pressured and pushed at your job, when the real pressures and pushes may be coming from circumstances beyond the job.

As I write these lines, I hear the clock chiming in the next room. The number of chimes tells me it's time to bring this writing session to a halt. If I don't, my life, including my life at work, will get out of balance. I can choose to keep writing. After all, I want to finish this manuscript. It's important to me. I can also choose to stop for the night.

The choice is mine. Which shall it be? I know myself fairly well. To keep working longer tonight will leave me too tired tomorrow to be at my best. So, I pause for the refreshment of rest and sleep in order to be able to work productively and with a measure of happiness in the coming day. The rhythm and balance of our lives—mine as well as yours—are important. Balancing other activities with work is necessary in order to be happier at work.

Balance Your Dreams and Your Work

One definition of the American way is as follows: *Make the most money possible—in an honest manner, of course; and seek the highest position available to you in your field of work.* Sound familiar? It's so familiar that to challenge, ignore, or sidestep this approach to life seems almost unpatriotic.

A source of much job unhappiness may lie in such an approach, however. Following this definition may lead a person into the wrong field and the wrong job. The job doesn't fit the person, the person doesn't fit the job. His or her competence is in other areas than this one.

The book *The Peter Principle* describes this problem with serious humor as it describes workers rising to their level of incompetence.[6] Unhappiness, or at least not as much happiness as there could be, is a part of the result of taking a job that pays well or offers prestige but the "fit" is not right.

Or maybe the problem is not lack of competence but the fact that the job somehow conflicts with one's deeply-held dreams and goals. An uncle of mine escaped this conflict and believed he had made the right choice. I believe he chose well, too. My uncle farmed for many years and then spent the last twenty years or so of his work life as a laborer in a paper mill. He drew wages, but he did not envy those who were salaried. He did not even envy those wage-earners who made more money by doing shift work, shifting around the clock from week to week, working two or three weekends a month. Far from it. He felt good about the pay he received. The work he did was honest and needed. He did it well. He maintained good relationships with those with whom he worked, too. They respected him, and he was their friend.

Even more, Uncle J.D.'s after-work time each day and on weekends was his. He could spend it doing carpentry as a hobby, playing with children, helping people, studying the Bible, and participating in the church he loved. Sometimes he just sat and whittled. His time beyond the work day was his to spend on the things in life he considered important.

Is a job more important than your dreams? That's for you to decide, of course. Certainly some dreams aren't worth dreaming, or they are too far afield from reality. As long as one is able, trying to fulfill any dream that doesn't include making enough money to support oneself and those people for whom one is responsible is foolish, immature, and, I believe, immoral. Such a selfish dream is really a fantasy, detached from reality.

Beware, though, of taking a job or a promotion only to fulfill another's dreams, even society's dreams. The *right* dream is more important than the *wrong* job.

Richard Bolles, a great helper of people through his leadership and writing on life/work planning and vocational guidance, suggests asking yourself this question: "What would you do if you had $10 million and you were required to spend it on yourself?"[7] List as many things as you can think of. Then ask yourself two more questions about each item you have listed. One, can you do this activity now, with the resources you have? Two, can you find or develop resources within the next five years to enable you to do this particular thing?[8]

Answering these questions yourself may reveal to you a little bit about your dreams and encourage you to begin to fulfill them. In the process you may well find ways to bring at least some of your dreams to reality through your job.

Personalizing This Idea

"Step right up. You pays your money, and you takes your choice." That's what the carnival barkers used to say. And it's still true about those areas in life over which we have a choice.

Remember, I'm agreeing with you that most people do not have control over as many aspects of their jobs as they would like, and this fact is a source of their unhappiness on the job. I'm also suggesting, though, that all of us have control over at least some areas of our jobs. My plea in this chapter is for you to exercise that control in such a way as to live with balance.

Within certain limitations, you, too, "pays your money and takes your choice" in balancing your work and your outside-of-work life, your outside-of-work activities and your work, and your dreams and your work. You'll need to choose what's important to you in each of these areas of balance.

Frankly you *have* chosen, and you *will* choose again. That is, right now, already, you've settled on a certain kind of balance, or lack of it, in your work and your life. Perhaps it's time to shift the weight of your on- and off-the-job activities in a new direction. Such an adjustment may enable you to realize a greater sense of happiness in the job you some-times just can't stand.

Key Points

1. Balance work and other activities.
2. Balance other activities and work.
3. Balance your dreams and your work.

Notes

1. Marsha Sinetar, *Do What You Love, the Money Will Follow* (New York: Paulist Press, 1987), 148.

2. Wayne E. Oates, *Confessions of a Workaholic: The Facts About Work Addiction* (New York: The World Publishing Company, 1971), 64-65.

3. Denis Waitley & Reni L. Witt, *The Joy of Working* (New York: Dodd, Mead & Company, 1985), 230.

4. Wayne E. Oates, *Your Right to Rest*, Potentials: Guides to Productive Living (Philadelphia: The Westminster Press, 1984), 63.

5. Ibid., 36.

6. Laurence Peter and Raymond Hull, *The Peter Principle* (New York: William Morrow & Company, Inc., 1969), 25.

7. Richard Nelson Bolles, *The Three Boxes of Life* (Berkeley, Calif.: Ten Speed Press, 1981), 447.

8. Ibid., 450.

10
Let Happiness Catch You

What, after all, is happiness? Norman Cousins, former editor of *Saturday Review*, has written, "Happiness is probably the easiest emotion to feel, the most elusive to create deliberately, and the most difficult to define. It is experienced differently by different people."[1] The fact that I agree with this statement is one reason I have saved until this last chapter any discussion of happiness itself. My hope is that as you have read the previous chapters you have attached your own description to the kind of happiness you desire.

Just to be clear about things, now is not the time to quibble about the difference between happiness and joy. For the sake of getting on with being happier, how about let's just agree to think of happiness and joy as meaning basically the same thing. It ought to be obvious that what we've been talking about in these pages is not anything on the surface. Rather, we've been talking about a real and substantial kind of happiness that certainly includes joy.

The renowned psychiatrist Rollo May wrote that " . . . joy is the emotion which accompanies our fulfilling our natures as human beings. It is based on the experience of one's identity as a being of worth and dignity . . . ."[2] Call it happiness or joy, achieving this reality in your life is what this book is about. We want to experience this reality in our work and in all the other areas of our lives. To put this thought in language that is more personal, you want to be the person that is uniquely you. And you want this unique you to be seen as being valuable and to be appreciated. You do not want to be considered as just a tool in a factory or an office—not even a highly-paid tool, although you wouldn't mind being paid more.

As you do the work, you want people to see that this is *you* doing the work. A robot or a monkey could *not* do this work with the same touch you give it. And furthermore, you want the work itself to do sufficient good to justify it being done, especially to justify your doing it. Too, you want to be rewarded sufficiently to enable you to assist yourself and those who depend on you to enjoy the commodities in life that require money.

Those desires are at least a part of the content of happiness on the job, in general. Specifically, though, nobody else can define the details of that happiness for you. Your happiness, and your idea of what happiness is, belong to you and you alone. Your definition of happiness is uniquely yours. That statement applies to the happiness you desire in and from your job as well as to the rest of the things you do and are.

As you search for your unique blend of experiences, feelings, and values that mean happiness for you, remember some principles that seem rather basic to everyone's happiness. Here are a few I know about. Let happiness catch you by putting these principles into practice.

Put Happiness Second

Don't put the search for happiness first in your life. Put happiness at least second, and maybe a good bit lower, on your scale of values, desires, and needs. The reason is simple. We don't get happiness when we seek it as our number one goal. Happiness always eludes us when we make it first on our list of priorities.

As Harold Kushner wrote in the best-selling book *When*

All You've Ever Wanted Isn't Enough, "Happiness is a butterfly—the more you chase it, the more it flies away from you and hides. But stop chasing it, put away your net and busy yourself with other, more productive things than the pursuit of happiness, and it will sneak up on you from behind and perch on your shoulder."[3]

Or consider the thought the wise older cat shared with the kitten who felt happiness was in his tail. The kitten kept chasing his tail round and round, unable to catch it, becoming more and more frustrated.

The wise older cat told him that he, too, believed that happiness was in a cat's tail. He had learned, however, that if he just stopped chasing his tail and gave himself to accomplishing the priorities of his life each day, something wonderful happened. Happiness followed him everywhere he went without his having to chase after it.

That's the tale of the tails. Now consider another tale. It's a classic Persian fairy tale, in fact. It's about three princes from the land of Serendip. The three princes set out in search of great treasures. They searched diligently, but they did not find the treasures they sought. What they found were treasures more magnificent than they had sought or even hoped for.

What the three princes of Serendip experienced is what we have come to call "serendipity." Serendipity applies to the experience of happiness. If we seek happiness directly, we miss it. We experience happiness when we place priority on other matters. In the case of finding happiness on the job, these "other matters" are the matters we've looked at in the previous pages.

Happiness on the job—or anywhere else—won't come if we brood about the fact that we're not as happy as we would like to be. Happiness comes only when we get out of our shells, do something about what we can do something about, and get on with life. When we do this, lots of times when we look around we find that happiness is following us. At least it's close by.

Stay Open to Happiness

Not seeking happiness as your first priority doesn't mean closing the door on happiness. Far from it. Although we won't find happiness by seeking it, we won't experience it by closing the door on it every chance we get either.

Give some folks a nearly-perfect item, and they'll find the flaw in it in a millionth of a second. The bolder flaw-finders will announce the flaw to everyone in earshot, too, giving all the details about the flaw and how they found it. These folks are perpetual fault-finders. They're experts at raining on parades, including their own. They examine everything and everyone. They look for hidden meanings in the most potentially positive announcements and actions. If anything is less than perfect, they'll find the imperfection, and that's what they will major on.

You won't find happiness by looking for the negative things of your job every day you go to work. Don't misunderstand. You don't need to close your eyes to the negatives. You don't need to deny that negatives exist. If you're going to be happier, however, you need to start focusing on the "up" experiences, not on the "downers."

Isn't anything good about the job you have? Then focus on those things, even one thing if that's all you can think of.

Some observers of people today suggest that one reason for the seemingly greater incidence of unhappiness is that our expectations are too high. One psychologist contrasts what he calls the "California self" to the "New England self." The "California self" focuses on the individual's wants and needs and feels that to an extent every experience ought to yield the maximum amount of satisfaction. A job must provide more than a living; it must also provide personal meaning, social good, excitement, and a large paycheck. The "New England self" is less preoccupied with individual desires and feelings about work or anything else.[4] (By the way, these descriptions are meant only to evoke an image rather than to exalt or deride any part of the country.)

I heartily confess that I kind of like that California self, too, else I wouldn't be concerned about being happier on the job. However, we let ourselves in for a good bit of unhappiness when we expect everything in life to yield unadulterated happiness, full and overflowing, all the time. It's not likely to happen.

Here's another thought along the same line. Dr. Theodore Rubin, well-known psychiatrist and author, said that he often makes this shocking statement to his patients: "What you've got now is probably as good as it's ever going to be."[5] He then goes on to explain that this doesn't mean that things can't get better and that the patient should not take initiative to make things better.

Dr. Rubin's point is that the patient already experiences a great many good things, more than many other human beings have the privilege of experiencing. He or she has the necessities of life, for one thing, and probably considerably more than that.

You yourself, by virtue of your existence in a modern culture, have a great many more material things, not to mention opportunities, than most people in our world. Life may not be as good as you want, as good as it can be, as good as you ought to expect, or as good as you ought to try to make it be. Life for most of us is likely pretty good in comparison to the life of many people in our world, however. Let's not give up in our quest for greater happiness, but let's recognize how fortunate we already are.

A Jewish folk tale describes a farmer who complained all of the time. He lived in a small room with his wife, two children, and a dog. The farmer was a very unhappy man. So he went to the rabbi and asked what he should do.

The rabbi asked the farmer whether he had a goat. The farmer replied that he did. The rabbi instructed the farmer to bring the goat in the house and come back and see him next week. The farmer went home, brought the goat inside, and returned to see the rabbi the next week. The rabbi asked the farmer how things were going. The farmer replied that things had gotten worse with the goat inside, along with his wife, two children, and a dog.

The farmer asked the rabbi what he should do next. The rabbi told him to bring in the cow. The next week the rabbi told the farmer to bring in the chickens. The fourth week the rabbi told the farmer to bring in the rabbits. The fifth week it was the horses.

The farmer's house now was filled with horses, rabbits, chickens, a cow, a goat, a dog, two children, and a wife. The farmer was not happy; instead, he was desperate.

The farmer told the rabbi he couldn't stand it anymore. "What should I do?" the farmer asked. The rabbi instructed him to get the horses out of his house. The next week, the rabbits; the next, the chickens.

Finally the man, his wife, two children, and the dog had the house to themselves again. The farmer went back to the rabbi. Before the rabbi could ask, the farmer told the rabbi how happy he was now.[6] He was only back where he started from when he went to the rabbi and complained about his lack of happiness.

Think, now. Isn't something good about your job? If you feel surrounded by a menagerie of animals of various sorts, at least rejoice that you don't have to work with *all* of the animals in the zoo! Maybe it's true that we appreciate even a little bit of happiness best when we can think how much worse things could be.

So, whatever good you can find in your job, focus on that. You may want to start keeping a diary of the things that make you happy on a given day. You can keep this diary on paper or in your mind, whichever option you think will help you to take the idea seriously.

As you look for the things that make you happy on a given day, don't look for the big things. Be happy that you can identify little things that give you even a little bit of happiness.

You may at first glance consider this suggestion to be simplistic and even a bit childish. I don't think it's childish, but it may well be childlike. Trying to identify even the smallest things that bring happiness can take us back to those moments of wonder and joy that we knew as children when we discovered things that now seem simple and ordinary to us. We make a mistake in our growing older if we let ourselves lose this ability to experience wonder. The most wondrous, joy-evoking experiences are often the simplest and most basic. The great researcher on stress, Hans Selye, put it like this: "The petty routine of daily problems also tends to blunt our sensitivity to the detached enjoyment of greatness and wonder. It is a pity that nowadays most people are so anxiously bent on being practical, on getting ahead in life, that they no longer find time to make sure where they really want to go. After a while, the prosperous businessman, the efficient administrator, the up-and-coming young lawyer begin to get that lost feeling of aimlessly drifting from day to day—toward retirement."[7]

So, try looking for the positive and the good in your job. At least be open to it. Guard against focusing on the negative elements all of the time.

You may be surprised at how the mind-set of looking for the good things, the things that bring happiness, can help you deal more positively with the problems your job contains. Some scientific evidence exists, in fact, to suggest that having a positive attitude has a chemical effect on the body that increases one's ability to deal with life and, in short, be happy.[8]

Personalizing This Idea

Put happiness second, not first, and so don't focus on happiness as the number one priority in your life. But stay open to happiness, even look for the good things, the positive things, the things that bring happiness.

These thoughts may appear contradictory at first glance, but I believe they are paradoxical, not contradictory. That is, they're both true. They're two sides of the same coin. Both thoughts are thus essential words of guidance if we are to let happiness catch us.

A person once owned a vast library of books. He had many favorite books in that library. One day he thought of one of these favorite books and began to search for it. He went down row upon row, shelf upon shelf, but he could not find it. The end of the day came and he still had not found that special book. He was unhappy and frustrated. He searched on into the night, growing more and more concerned that he could not find this special, particularly enjoyable book. Finally he grew exhausted and fell into a troubled, rest-less sleep.

No, a princess did not come and tell him where to find the book. He awakened the next morning and grouchily began searching anew for the book. As he searched, he saw many books that were meaningful and enjoyable to him. But he tossed these books aside, growling and grumbling all the while.

Some of the books he tossed aside were every bit as enjoyable and as special to him as this book for which he was searching. But he was not thinking of any book but the one he was seeking.

So, he kept searching, all the while growing more and more unhappy, if that's possible. He could not find that special book. He looked through the whole library and could not find *that* book. He sat down and cried. That's pretty much the end of the story.

I kid you not, but there was another person who had a vast library. This person's library was every bit as vast and as potentially enjoyable and special as the library of the guy I just told you about.

This second person with the vast library began to think one day about a special book in her library. She said to herself, "I think I'll try to find that book." And so she set out to find it.

As she started down the first row of her library, though, a book title caught her eye. Instantly her mind flooded with happiness. "Ha, ha, ha," she chuckled to herself.

She recalled reading that book and thought for a moment about the joy it had brought her as she read it. She picked up the book, turned to a familiar page, read a few humorous paragraphs, and laughed and laughed and laughed. I can't tell you for sure how long she laughed, but it was a long time.

She went to the next shelf. Another book title caught her eye. She had not read this book. She glanced at the table of contents and then started in on the first chapter. It was a great book, too! She had always meant to read it, and now was her chance. She read and read and read and enjoyed and enjoyed and enjoyed and laughed and laughed and laughed. A lot.

Well, I could tell you more of her happy story. There's lots more, in fact, but maybe you get the idea.

Who would you like to be like? It's pretty much up to you. It's your happiness that's at stake. Why don't you let happiness, instead of something else, catch you?

Key Points

1. Put happiness second.
2. Stay open to happiness.

Notes

1. Dennis Wholey, *Discovering Happiness: Personal Conversations About Getting the Most Out of Life* (New York: Avon Books, 1986), xv.

2. Rollo May, *Man's Search for Himself* (New York: W. W. Norton & Company, Inc., 1953), 96.

3. Harold Kushner, *When All You've Ever Wanted Isn't Enough* (New York: Pocket Books, 1986), 23.

4. Martin E. P. Seligman, "Boomer Blues," *Psychology Today*, XXII (October 1988), 52.

5. Wholey, *Discovering Happiness*, 47.

6. Ibid., 157.

7. Hans Selye, *The Stress of Life*, revised edition (New York: McGraw-Hill Book Co., 1976), 443-444.

8. Denis Waitley & Reni L. Witt, *The Joy of Working* (New York: Dodd, Mead & Company, 1985), 18-19.

Postscript:
What If None of These Ideas
Make Enough Difference

The summer prior to my son's senior year in college, he went to Japan and studied in a Japanese language institute. He lived with a fine Japanese family. In fact, he really became an unofficial member of that family for a summer. He referred to the Japanese parents as his mother and father, and he called the children of that family his sisters and brothers.

During the course of that summer, he adjusted quite well to eating many things the Japanese people eat. Once when he called home, he reported to us a Japanese recipe for fish. "First," he said, "you take a fish." He paused, and we waited to hear the rest of the recipe. Then he said, "That's it!" Quite a recipe! He referred to the Japanese custom, of course, of eating fish raw.

You may question how the ideas in this book will really help you be happier in your job as much as I question the idea of eating raw fish. If eating raw fish is my only choice for survival or is necessary for courtesy's sake, I've found I can do it. I might even say I like it. Really, though, if I have a reasonable option, I'd just as soon not eat raw fish.

What about the ideas in this book? Will they work for you? I hope that at least one of them will, and I hope you will give one or more of these ideas enough of a try to see whether they really will help you in your particular job. I truly believe these ideas *will* help you, and I encourage you to put them into practice for a reasonable period of time.

But what if they don't work? Or what if they don't help you enough? What if your miserableness overwhelms your live possibilities for increasing your happiness in your job? What if your job continues to be a whole lot like eating raw fish and you just can't tolerate it, much less like it?

Open Your Eyes to Your Options

I like what I heard humorist Roy Blount, Jr., say on the last live broadcast of the radio show "Prairie Home Companion." As I recall hearing it, he shared this bit of wisdom:
"It's better for something to be good and over
    Than rotten and still going strong."[1]
What that may mean for you and your job is simple. Since even the best things can go sour and need to come to an end, there may well come a time when you ought boldly to look for a way out of a work situation that seems intolerable to you. Maybe the job was good for you once, but no more. Maybe there's another job that's more compatible with your abilities, interests, and needs.

To spend one's life beating one's head against a brick wall is not what a relatively normal person would choose to do if another option were available. If you've done your best over a reasonable period of time (Six months? A year? Longer? Shorter? Your decision.) to be happier in the job you sometimes can't stand and things don't seem to be getting much better, maybe it's time to look for other pastures.

These "other pastures" may not be greener, but at least they will be different. And that may help, in itself.

A good bit of what real life is about is seeking the particular set of problems that best fit your abilities to handle them. That may seem to be a bit cynical to some, but I think such an outlook is quite realistic.

The pastures elsewhere may not be greener. You *won't* find the perfect job. It's not likely you will, that is. Indeed, the next job is not guaranteed to be *any* better. Some things about the next job may, in fact, be worse. What you may find in a new job, though, is a set of problems that more nearly fit the solutions you can offer than the set of problems with which you are dealing now.

Sometimes taking the risk for better or worse is just what has to be done. You'll have to decide whether things are bad enough to take the risk.

Making a change need not suggest that anything is really wrong with your present job and certainly not that anything at all is wrong with you. The match of your job and you is simply not right. For other people, your job may be the best thing since sliced bread. For you, it's a whole lot less than desirable. The problem is the match—not the job, not you, but the match of the job and you.

Take the matter of the stressful aspect of your present job, for instance. People can handle different amounts and different kinds of stress. If your job generates too much stress of the wrong kind for you to deal with in a healthy manner, that may well be a signal to you to seek the kind of job that is a better match.[2]

A bit of classic Southern spiritual wisdom goes like this: "When your burden gets too heavy, lay it down, lay it down."[3] If you've done everything else you can think of— including applying the ideas in this book—to gain greater happiness, maybe laying the burden down is the next thing to do. Maybe the burden of your present job doesn't fit you, and you need to find one that more nearly does.

Start Looking at the Possibilities

You may need to learn to be versatile in your job search. I recently saw a newspaper clipping about a person in a Southern state who was a bartender at Sally's Beauty Shop and Chain Saw Repair. (Could that be true? True or not, it was definitely in the newspaper. Name changed, though, to protect the innocent, including me.) One would think the person who filled that job would have to have multiple talents, to say the least. I have the feeling that she (or he?) could handle just about any situation.

Maybe you are just as versatile, just as gifted, and even more so. But, do be careful out there as you look for the job-changing possibilities. You need to evaluate yourself and your job-changing possibilities carefully.

What are your options? If you can think of more than these, more power to you:

(1) You might change jobs in your current company.

(2) You might change employers within your same career field.

(3) You might change careers entirely.

(4) You might become your own boss by going into business for yourself.

Options (1) and (2), changing jobs in your company and changing employers within your present career field, are probably the easiest to pull off. Choosing these options may well be the most satisfying answer if you are happy in your current career field.

A respected career counselor suggests, "Most men and women do not need to quit their employers in order to enjoy job satisfaction."[4] Maybe you fit in that "most." Another veteran career counselor states emphatically, "You should not quit a job until you have explored and exhausted every possibility of opportunity where you are."[5] If you have options for movement in your company, you may be able to find a better match in another position with your present employer. You should explore this possibility carefully before considering the second option.

Option (2), changing employers within your present career field is next in the order of difficulty, generally. Choosing this option enables you to use the resources, contacts, education, experience, and achievements you already have.

Option (3), changing career fields, is more difficult. An experienced, capable career counselor tells how people who have been in a certain career for fifteen or twenty years will sometimes decide to change careers. Changing careers seems quite romantic and exciting. However, many will find that changing careers requires entering a training program for that career. Next they find that they may have to start at the bottom of the ladder for that career. They may still press on, invest the resources required, and make the change. Sometimes the change works, and sometimes it doesn't. Even when the change turns out to be worthwhile, the person might have been just as happy taking the less drastic step of shifting jobs within a given career field.[6]

Option (4)—going into business for yourself—is also a more risky venture than options (1) and (2), of course. For most such ventures, capital—money—is required. And, you must be prepared to invest plenty of time and energy. Making the change won't be easy, however much going into business for yourself appeals to you.

Only you can decide which of these options is the best for you. Telling you which is best for you, or even giving you much guidance in making the choice, is beyond the scope of this book. You need to talk to some trusted friends, and you need to do some research on your own. Some good books are available, and you ought to do your homework by reading some of them. I'll list a few good ones in this note, in case you're interested.[7]

It's Your Move Now

It always has been your move, in fact. That's the basic idea behind most of the other ideas in this book.

You're free to look for other options than the job you have, and you're free to make the best of your current job. It's your move.

An employee was talking with a friend about his lack of

happiness in his job. He said, "I feel like a bird in a cage." The friend replied with telling insight, "The door is open."[8] The door is open for you, too. Maybe it's open only a crack. Maybe it's open a good bit wider. Maybe you'll need to exert the energy to open it wider. The point is, it's open enough that it's your move now. You can choose to make the best of the job you have. Or you can look for other options. It's your move. What are you waiting for?

Key Points

1. Open your eyes to the options.
2. Start looking at the possibilities.
3. It's your move now.

Notes

1. Roy Blount, Jr., on "Prairie Home Companion," June 13, 1987, broadcast on the American Public Radio Network.

2. Vernon E. Buck, *Working Under Pressure* (New York: Crane, Russak & Company, Inc., 1972), 181.

3. Source unknown; public domain.

4. Bernard Haldane, *Career Satisfaction and Success: A Guide to Job Freedom* (New York: AMACOM, 1974), 11.

5. Ibid., 89.

6. Jean Lisette Brodey, *Mid-Life Careers* (Philadelphia: Bridgebooks, The Westminster Press, 1983), 70-71.

7. If you can find or buy only one book that will help in the area of career decisions, get the latest annual edition of this one (it's updated each year): Richard Nelson Bolles, *What Color Is Your Parachute? A Practical Manual for Job-Hunters & Career Changers*, 1990 Edition (Berkeley, Calif.: Ten Speed Press, 1990).

For further help, you'll find lots of books available. These are among the good ones, their value to you depending on your needs, interests, and inclinations:

Richard Nelson Bolles, *The Three Boxes of Life and How to Get Out of*

Them: An Introduction to Life/Work Planning (Berkeley, Calif.: Ten Speed Press, 1981).

Jean Lisette Brodey, *Mid-Life Careers* (Philadelphia: Bridgebooks, The Westminster Press, 1983).

Bernard Haldane, *Career Satisfaction and Success: A Guide to Job Freedom* (New York: AMACOM, 1974).

8. Patricia King, *Never Work for a Jerk!* (New York: Dell Publishing, 1987), 334.

Selected Bibliography

Albrecht, Karl. *Brain Power.* Englewood Cliffs, N. J.: Prentice-Hall, Inc., 1980.

Anderson, Walter. *Courage Is a Three-Letter Word.* New York: Fawcett Crest, 1986.

Blanchard, Kenneth, and Norman Vincent Peale. *The Power of Ethical Management.* New York: William Morrow and Company, Inc., 1988.

Blanchard, Marjorie, and Mark J. Tager. *Working Well: Managing for Health and High Performance.* New York: Simon and Schuster, 1985.

Bolles, Richard Nelson. *The Three Boxes of Life and How to Get Out of Them: An Introduction to Life/Work Planning.* Berkeley, Calif.: Ten Speed Press, 1981.

_____. *What Color Is Your Parachute? A Practical Manual for Job-Hunters & Career Changers.* 1990 Edition. Berkeley, Calif.: Ten Speed Press, 1990.

Brodey, Jean Lisette. *Mid-Life Careers.* Philadelphia: Bridgebooks, The Westminster Press, 1983.

Buck, Vernon E. *Working Under Pressure.* New York: Crane-Russak Company, 1972.

Cadenhead, Jr., Al. *Hurry Up and Rest.* Nashville, Tenn.: Broadman Press, 1988.

Carnegie, Dale. *How to Enjoy Your Life and Your Job: Selections from How to Win Friends and Influence People and How to Stop Worrying and Start Living.* New York: Pocket Books, 1985.

Dittes, James E. *When Work Goes Sour.* Philadelphia: The Westminster Press, 1987.

Everly, Dr. George S., Jr., and Dr. Daniel A. Girdano. *The Stress Mess Solution: The Causes and Cures of Stress on the Job.* Bowie, Md.: Robert J. Brady Co., A Prentice-Hall Company, 1980.

Forbes, Rosalind. *Corporate Stress.* Garden City, New York: Doubleday & Company, 1979.

Germann, Richard, Diane Blumenson, and Peter Arnold. *Working and*

Liking It. New York: Fawcett Gold Medal, 1984.

Grove, Andrew S. *High Output Management*. New York: Random House, 1983.

Haldane, Bernard. *Career Satisfaction and Success: A Guide to Job Freedom*. New York: AMACOM, 1974.

Hersey, Paul, and Kenneth Blanchard. *Managing Organizational Behavior: Utilizing Human Resources*. Second edition. Englewood Cliffs, N. J.: Prentice-Hall, Inc., 1972.

Herzberg, Frederick. *Work and the Nature of Man*. Cleveland: The World Publishing Company, 1966.

Kushner, Harold. *When All You've Ever Wanted Isn't Enough*. New York: Pocket Books, 1986.

Lakein, Alan. *How to Get Control of Your Time and Your Life*. New York: Wyden, 1973.

Levering, Robert. *A Great Place to Work*. New York: Random House, 1988.

Maccoby, Michael. *Why Work: Leading the New Generation*. New York: Simon and Schuster, 1988.

Minirth, Frank B., M.D., and Paul D. Meier, M.D. *Happiness Is a Choice: A Manual on the Symptoms, Causes, and Cures of Depression*. Grand Rapids, Michigan: Baker Book House, 1988.

Oates, Wayne E. *Confessions of a Workaholic: The Facts About Work Addiction*. New York: The World Publishing Company, 1971.

_____. *Your Right to Rest*. Potentials: Guides to Productive Living. Philadelphia: The Westminster Press, 1984.

Rosow, Jerome M. *The Worker and the Job*. An American Assembly Book. Englewood Cliffs, N. J.: Prentice-Hall, Inc., 1974.

Russianoff, Penelope. *When Am I Going to Be Happy?: How to Break the Emotional Bad Habits That Make You Miserable*. Toronto: Bantam Books, 1988.

Selye, Hans. *The Stress of Life*. Revised edition. New York: McGraw-Hill Book Co., 1976.

Sinetar, Marsha. *Do What You Love, the Money Will Follow*. New York: Paulist Press, 1987.

Terkel, Studs. *Working: People Talk About What They Do All Day and How They Feel About What They Do*. New York: Pantheon Books, 1974.

Uris, Auren. *Thank God It's Monday*. New York: Thomas Y. Crowell Company, 1974.

Waitley, Denis. *Seeds of Greatness: The Ten Best-Kept Secrets of Total Success*. Old Tappan, N. J.: Spire Books, Fleming H. Revell Company, 1983.

Waitley, Denis, and Reni L. Witt. *The Joy of Working.* New York: Dodd, Mead & Company, 1985.

Wholey, Dennis. *Discovering Happiness: Personal Conversations About Getting the Most Out of Life.* New York: Avon Books, 1986.